MW00437316

CHOOSE LIFE NOT DEATH!

JESUS CHRIST PROCLAIMED – "I AM THE RESURRECTION AND THE LIFE. AND WHO SO EVER LIVETH AND BELIEVETH IN ME SHALL NEVER DIE. DO YOU BELIEVE ME? *BELIEVE AND RECEIVE.*"
JOHN 11

PASTOR JAMES HEATON III

chooselifenotdeath.com

1

THIS IS A HOW-TO BOOK OF LIFE, LOVE, AND ACCEPTANCE. EVERY BELIEVER IN JESUS CHRIST WHO HAS TRULY BECOME ONE WITH HIM IN ETERNAL LIFE, BY THE POWER OF THE HOLY SPIRIT CAN WALK WITH JESUS CHRIST IN HIS MIRACLES OF LOVE AND RESTORATION. YOU ARE EITHER IN LIFE OR IN DEATH ALL THE TIME. THIS BOOK WILL TEACH YOU HOW TO BECOME ONE WITH JESUS CHRIST, AS HE IS ONE WITH THE FATHER, LIVE IN LIFE, ETERNAL LIFE ON EARTH AS IT IS IN HEAVEN AND OVERCOME THE SPIRIT OF DEATH. **YOU HAVE AUTHORITY OVER DEATH. DEATH HAS NO HOLD ON YOU!**

BLESSINGS,

JESUS CHRIST THE ANSWER ETERNAL LIFE

PASTOR JAMES

**THS: REVELATIONS OF THE HOLY SPIRIT GIVEN TO PASTOR JAMES

TABLE OF CONTENTS

3

5

WELCOME TO THE REVOLUTION OF LIFE, LOVE & ACCEPTANCE, CHOOSE LIFE NOT DEATH!

THE TIME IS NOW FOR THE REVOLUTION OF THE TRUTH. WHAT YOU ARE ABOUT TO EXPERIENCE WILL ENLIGHTEN YOU AND ALL OF CHRISTIANITY TO WHAT IS REAL AND WHAT IS NOT REAL, TO WHAT IS TRUE AND WHAT IS NOT TRUE. PREPARE YOURSELF FOR YOUR LIFE TO CHANGE AS NEVER BEFORE. **GOD CREATED ALL OF CREATION. GOD HAS TOTAL AUTHORITY OVER ALL OF CREATION, CREATION HAS NO AUTHORITY OVER GOD. GOD CREATED THE EARTH AND TOOK PART OF THE EARTH AND CREATED ADAM AND FILLED HIM WITH HIS HOLY SPIRIT, THE BREATH OF LIFE, AND REVEALED HIS KNOWLEDGE TO HIM AND GAVE HIM DOMINION OVER THE EARTH. ADAM SINNED, (FELL INTO AGREEMENT WITH THE DEVIL, THE SPIRIT OF DEATH), AND GAVE HIS DOMINION OF THE EARTH OVER TO THE DEVIL. THIS IS GOD'S REVELATION OF HIS TRUTH, THE TRUE GOSPEL MESSAGE OF THE KINGDOM, OF HOW AND WHY HE SENT HIS SON, JESUS CHRIST, TO TAKE BACK DOMINION OF THE EARTH FROM THE DEVIL AND REDEEM MANKIND AND ALL OF CREATION. JESUS CHRIST CAME IN THE FLESH TO THIS EARTH AS A BABY BOY. HE DIED ON THE CROSS TO SET US FREE FROM OUR SIN. HE AROSE FROM THE GRAVE, TOOK DOMINION OF THE EARTH AWAY FROM THE DEVIL, AND TOLD US, HIS PEOPLE, TO TAKE DOMINION UNTIL HE COMES AGAIN FOR US. NOW WHEN WE BECOME ONE WITH JESUS CHRIST, AS HE IS ONE WITH THE FATHER, TRUE SON'S AND DAUGHTER'S, MADE IN THE IMAGE OF GOD, SEATED IN HEAVENLY PLACES, FILLED WITH THE HOLY SPIRIT, HE GIVES US HIS POWER AND AUTHORITY TO USE HIS NAME, (POWER OF ATTORNEY), OVER CREATION. REMEMBER, GOD CREATED THE ANGEL WHO BECAME THE DEVIL, THE SPIRIT OF DEATH. WHEN WE BECOME ONE WITH JESUS CHRIST, THE CREATOR OF EVERYTHING, WE HAVE POWER AND AUTHORITY OVER THE DEVIL, THE SPIRIT OF DEATH, AND ANYTHING THAT**

DEALS WITH DEATH, SUCH AS SICKNESS, DISEASE, AGEING, POVERTY, ETC. AND OVER THE NATURAL REALM THAT HE, JESUS CHRIST, CREATED!

THIS REVELATION OF TWO SCIPTURES IS GOING TO SET YOU ON FIRE. MAT. 16-27, 28.

"FOR THE SON OF MAN SHALL COME IN THE GLORY OF HIS FATHER WITH HIS ANGELS; AND THEN HE SHALL REWARD EVERY MAN ACCORDING TO HIS WORKS. VERILY I SAY UNTO YOU, THERE BE SOME STANDING HERE, WHICH SHALL NOT TASTE OF DEATH, TILL THEY SEE THE SON OF MAN COMING IN HIS KINGDOM." HALLELUJAH! NOW YOU KNOW THAT THERE ARE PEOPLE OF GOD LIVING ON THIS EARTH THAT ARE OVER 2000 YEARS OLD -PROOF- OF ETERNAL LIFE ON EARTH AS IT IS IN HEAVEN. BELIEVE AND RECEIVE WHAT THE SPIRIT OF JESUS CHRIST, THE SPIRIT OF ETERNAL LIFE, IS SPEAKING FORTH TO YOU.

THIS BOOK WILL HELP TEACH YOU HOW TO BECOME ONE WITH JESUS CHRIST AS HE IS ONE WITH THE FATHER AND IN JESUS NAME TAKE AUTHORITY OVER THE DEVIL, THE SPIRIT OF DEATH, AND ALL OF NATURAL CREATION. HOLD ON FOR THE LIGHT OF THE REVELATION OF JESUS CHRIST TO RESTORE ALL IN ALL IN YOU AND THROUGH HIS TRUTH IN YOU SET HIS PEOPLE FREE.

NEWS FLASH: THE SPIRIT OF DEATH HAS BEEN EXPOSED!

NEWS FLASH: JESUS CHRIST THE ANSWER ETERNAL LIFE CAME IN THE FLESH, AND HE HAS OVERCOME THE SPIRIT OF DEATH!

NEWS FLASH: WHEN YOU BECOME ONE WITH JESUS CHRIST, HE GIVES YOU HIS POWER AND AUTHORITY TO OVERCOME THE SPIRIT OF DEATH, YOU HAVE AUTHORITY OVER DEATH, DEATH HAS NO HOLD ON YOU!

THE TRUE ENEMY OF ALL MANKIND, OF ALL CREATION, HAS BEEN REVEALED AND NOW IS EXPOSED AND CAN NO LONGER HIDE. YOU MUST KNOW WHO YOUR ENEMY IS TO DEFEAT HIM. THE TRUE ENEMY IS THE SPIRIT OF DEATH! THE BLINDNESS OF THE SPIRIT OF DEATH HAS BEEN HANDED DOWN THROUGH THE GENERATIONS. WE ARE SERIOUSLY BEGINNING TO REAP WHAT WE HAVE SOWN. IT IS TIME FOR THIS LIE TO BE REVEALED AND OVERCOME BY THE SPIRIT OF LIFE, THE TRUTH OF JESUS CHRIST THE ANSWER ETERNAL LIFE.

MISSION: TO SOW THE SPIRIT OF LIFE, JESUS CHRIST THE ANSWER ETERNAL LIFE INTO ALL THE WORLD, AND SET FREE ALL OF CREATION FROM THE SPIRIT OF DEATH!

JESUS CHRIST MADE A WAY WHERE THERE WAS NO WAY! THANKS TO JESUS, THERE IS MORE THAN A WAY OUT! JESUS CHRIST THE ANSWER ETERNAL LIFE!

THIS IS A HOW-TO MANUAL OF LIFE, LOVE, AND ACCEPTANCE, BASED ON THE HOLY BIBLE, THE LIVING WORD OF GOD, AND REVELATIONS OF THE HOLY SPIRIT. GOD'S WISDOM OF HOW TO BECOME TRUE SONS AND DAUGHTERS OF GOD, MANIFESTING HIS HOLINESS AND OVERCOMING THE SPIRIT OF DEATH WITH THE SPIRIT OF LIFE, ETERNAL LIFE ON EARTH AS IT IS IN HEAVEN.

WE CHRISTIANS HAVE ALLOWED THE SPIRIT OF DEATH TO BOMBARD AND BECOME PERVASIVE THROUGHOUT OUR ENTIRE CULTURE – OUR CHURCHES, BUSINESS, POLITICS, SPORTS, TV, RADIO, INTERNET, MUSIC, SOCIAL MEDIAS, SCHOOLS, ETC – ALL ARE PUSHING US TOWARDS A COVENANT WITH DEATH - OUR

BABIES, YOUTH, AND NOW OUR ADULTS ARE PAYING THE PRICE! WE MUST STOP THIS ONSLAUGHT OF DEATH, AND THERE IS ONLY ONE ANSWER, CHOOSE LIFE NOT DEATH! JESUS CHRIST – THE ANSWER – ETERNAL LIFE!

NOW WE MUST GRASP A HOLD OF THIS OBVIOUS FACT, OUR YOUNG LADIES AND MEN ARE THE FUTURE MOTHERS AND FATHERS OF OUR NATION AND THE WORLD. WE, AS ADULT CHRISTIANS ARE TO PROTECT THEM AND TEACH THEM. OUR FIRST RESPONSIBILITY IS TO BREAK OFF THE SPIRIT OF DEATH OPPRESSING THEM, AND TEACH THEM THE TRUTH OF JESUS CHRIST. HOW HIS TRUE LOVE IN US, HIS POWER AND AUTHORITY IN US, MAKES US OVERCOMERS OVER THE SPIRIT OF DEATH AND HOW TO BECOME SPIRITUAL WARRIORS, HOW TO BREAK OFF THE SPIRIT OF DEATH OFF OF THEMSELVES, OTHERS, AND THEIR FUTURE CHILDREN. HOW TO SET **ALL OF CREATION** FREE!

THE FIRST LESSON IS THAT GOD IS GOD, AND EVERYTHING HE DOES IS FOR OUR BENEFIT, NOT FOR HIS. GOD IS THE SPIRIT OF LIFE, ETERNAL LIFE, AND THE DEVIL IS THE SPIRIT OF DEATH, ETERNAL DEATH. FROM THIS MOMENT FORWARD REALIZE EVERYTIME YOU HEAR THE WORD GOD, THINK SPIRIT OF LIFE, AND EVERYTIME YOU HEAR THE WORD DEVIL, THINK SPIRIT OF DEATH. YOU HAVE TO KNOW WHO YOUR ENEMY IS TO DEFEAT HIM. **NOW, NEVER FORGET THIS FACT, THE DEVIL, (THE SPIRIT OF DEATH), A CREATED BEING, IS TOTALLY DEFEATED BY JESUS CHRIST, AND WHEN YOU BECOME ONE WITH HIM SEATED IN HEAVENLY PLACES, HE GIVES YOU HIS AUTHORITY OVER THE SPIRIT OF DEATH.**

THE FOLLOWING ARE GOD'S REVELATIONS FOR YOU.

JESUS CHRIST'S DNA - SPIRIT OF LIFE, ETERNAL LIFE

FAITH - AGREEMENT WITH JESUS CHRIST / AGREEMENT WITH SPIRIT OF LIFE
DEVIL'S DNA - SPIRIT OF DEATH, ETERNAL DEATH
SIN - AGREEMENT WITH THE SPIRIT OF DEATH
DEVIL OPPRESSION - SPIRIT OF DEATH
DEVIL POSSESSION - SPIRIT OF ETERNAL DEATH

THESE ARE THREE WAYS THAT GOD SETS YOU FREE FROM SIN.

1. THE BREATH OF THE HOLY SPIRIT, THE LANGUAGE OF ETERNAL LIFE, BREAKS AND OVERCOMES ALL OPPRESSION, OF THE SPIRIT OF DEATH, AND MAKES WAY FOR THE SPIRIT OF LIFE TO ENTER IN!

2. BAPTISM WASHES AWAY ALL SIN, WASHES AWAY SPIRIT OF DEATH, AND MAKES WAY FOR THE SPIRIT OF LIFE TO ENTER IN!

3. COMMUNION WASHES AWAY ALL SIN, WASHES AWAY SPIRIT OF DEATH, AND MAKES WAY FOR THE SPIRIT OF LIFE TO ENTER IN!

NOW, THAT YOUR EYES HAVE BEEN OPENED TO THE TRUTH, HERE COMES GOD'S HOLY LIVING ANSWER TO SET YOU FREE!

THE HEAVENLY ANGELS PROCLIAMED:
PEACE ON EARTH – GOODWILL TOWARD MEN LUKE 2

LIFE AND PEACE ARE PRICELESS!

JESUS CHRIST IS THE SOURCE OF ALL CREATION, LIFE, ETERNAL LIFE, LOVE, PEACE, AND JOY! JESUS CHRIST IS THE ONLY WAY YOU

WILL EVER HAVE LIFE, ETERNAL LIFE, TRUE LOVE, PEACE, AND JOY!

NOW, LISTEN CAREFULLY TO THE HEART OF JESUS CHRIST, HIS INNERMOST FEELINGS FOR YOU. TRUST ME, I LOVE ALL OF YOU THE SAME, CONFESS AND REPENT OF YOUR SIN, GET OUT OF AGREEMENT WITH THE DEVIL, THE SPIRIT OF DEATH, STOP BELIEVING THE LIES OF DEATH, AND GET INTO AGREEMENT WITH ME, TRUTH, THE SPIRIT OF LIFE. LET ME LOVE ON YOU, FORGIVE YOU, RESTORE YOU, EMPOWER YOU, AND SET YOU FREE TO ETERNAL LIFE. LET ME GIVE YOU MY PEACE, AND MY JOY. LET ME COVER YOU WITH MY AMAZING GRACE. COME HOME TO YOUR FIRST LOVE, BECOME ONE WITH ME AND I WILL GIVE YOU MY REST, ETERNAL LIFE ON EARTH AS IT IS IN HEAVEN. BELIEVE AND RECEIVE, "I AM THE WAY THE TRUTH AND THE LIFE, AND NO MAN COMETH UNTO THE FATHER BUT BY ME". JN 14 CHOOSE LIFE NOT DEATH!

VIP! YOU ARE NOW BEING BLESSED WITH THE TRUTH OF JESUS CHRIST AND ONLY HIS TRUTH WILL SET YOU FREE. JN 8 IF THE SON, JESUS CHRIST, SETS YOU FREE, YOU SHALL BE FREE INDEED. JN8 JESUS CHRIST IS GENTLE, TENDER, LOVING AND HE WILL NEVER FORCE HIMSELF UPON YOU AND HE WILL NEVER FORCE YOU TO DO ANYTHING AGAINST YOUR WILL. YOU MUST ASK HIM FOR EVERYTHING THAT YOU WANT, AND ALLOW HIM TO GIVE IT TO YOU, ASK AND IT SHALL BE GIVEN YOU, SEEK AND YOU WILL FIND, KNOCK, AND IT SHALL BE OPENED UNTO YOU. JN 7 NOW YOU MUST LET YOURSELF GO, GIVE YOURSELF TO HIM, QUIT HOLDING ON TO YOUR SIN, AGREEMENT WITH THE SPIRIT OF DEATH, KNOW THAT JESUS CHRIST DEEMS YOU WORTHY AND THAT HE WANTS TO GIVE YOU YOUR ANSWER MORE THAN YOU WANT IT, JESUS CHRIST, THE ANSWER, ETERNAL LIFE.

THE KEY: LEARN TO LOVE, LEARN TO ACCEPT LOVE, AND LEARN TO LOVE AND ACCEPT EACH OTHER INTO THE KINGDOM OF GOD. CHOOSE LIFE NOT DEATH! JOHN 15

THE KEY TO STAYING IN AGREEMENT WITH JESUS CHRIST, ABIDING IN HIS PRESENCE, AND OPERATING IN HIS MIRACLES OF LOVE, IS THE FOLLOWING:

DAILY READ YOUR BIBLE...
TRUST, OBEY, AND ACT ON GOD'S HOLY LIVING WORD OF TRUTH.

DAILY CONFESS AND REPENT...

"JESUS CHRIST, I CONFESS AND REPENT OF MY SIN (AGREEMENT WITH THE SPIRIT OF DEATH), THAT WOULD KEEP YOU FROM ABIDING IN ME AND ME FROM ABIDING IN YOU. HOLY SPIRIT, JESUS CHRIST, FATHER GOD, CLEANSE ME OF ALL UNRIGHTEOUSNESS, SET ME FREE, GIVE ME YOUR PEACE, LIFT ME INTO YOUR PRESENCE, INTO YOUR MARVELOUS LIGHT, INTO ETERNAL LIFE ON EARTH AS IT IS IN HEAVEN. THE SAME LOVE THAT CREATED ME IS RESTORING ME NOW, RESTORATION OF ALL IN ALL AS IF IT NEVER HAPPENED. THANK YOU JESUS FOR SETTING ME FREE."

DAILY COMMUNION...

JESUS CHRIST MADE A WAY WHERE THERE WAS NO WAY.
TO BECOME **ONE** WITH JESUS CHRIST, HE INSTITUTED
COMMUNION WITH HIS OWN BODY AND HIS OWN BLOOD
TO SET YOU FREE. THE HOLY SPIRIT, THROUGH
COMMUNION, LIFTS YOU UP INTO HIS PRESENCE AND SEATS
YOU IN HEAVENLY PLACES, ETERNAL LIFE. THIS
COMMUNION IS BETWEEN YOU AND JESUS CHRIST ONLY!
NO PASTOR OR PRIEST IS REQUIRED. ALSO, ANY FOOD AND
DRINK IS ACCEPTABLE.

"THIS IS HIS BODY, THE BREAD OF LIFE, BROKEN FOR ME,
AND THIS IS HIS BLOOD, THE BLOOD OF THE NEW
COVENANT, THE ETERNAL LIFE COVENANT, A FRESH
TRANSFUSION OF GOD'S DNA, WASHES AWAY THE SPIRIT OF
DEATH, AND GIVES ME AUTHORITY OVER DEATH. THANK
YOU JESUS FOR SETTING ME FREE."

DAILY TESTIMONY...

"I AM A NEW CREATURE FILLED WITH THE HOLY SPIRIT OF
ALMIGHTY GOD, THE SPIRIT OF ETERNAL LIFE, SEATED IN
HEAVENLY PLACES WITH JESUS CHRIST, MY LORD AND
SAVIOR. I AM NOT SUBJECT TO NATURAL LAW, NATURAL
LAW IS SUBJECT TO ME. I AM NOT OF THIS WORLD, **I HAVE
AUTHORITY OVER DEATH, *DEATH HAS NO HOLD ON ME*.** I
AM A TRUE SON OR DAUGHTER OF GOD, MADE IN THE
IMAGE OF GOD, LOVED, ACCEPTED, AND RESTORED WITH
ETERNAL LIFE ON EARTH AS IT IS IN HEAVEN. I AM GOING
TO LIVE ON THIS EARTH HEALTHY, WHOLE, PROSPEROUS,
BLESSED, REGENERATED AND RESTORED, IN LOVE, PEACE,
AND JOY, SPIRIT, SOUL AND BODY BLAMELESS, UNTIL JESUS
RETURNS. AND HE WILL FIND ME SOWING THE SPIRIT OF

13

LIFE, JESUS CHRIST THE ANSWER ETERNAL LIFE INTO ALL THE WORLD, AND SETTING FREE ALL OF CREATION FROM THE SPIRIT OF DEATH, AND THEN I AM GOING TO LIVE, RULE AND REIGN WITH HIM FOREVER. THANK YOU JESUS FOR SETTING ME FREE! AMEN!"

WHAT YOU HAVE JUST PROCLAIMED IS VERY, VERY IMPORTANT. ONCE YOU HAVE OVERCOME THE SPIRIT OF DEATH, THE ENTIRE SPIRITUAL REALM IS WAITING FOR YOUR NEXT WORDS. THESE WORDS, THIS PROCLAMATION SEALS THE DEAL WITH JESUS AND SHUTS OUT THE SPIRIT OF DEATH. REALIZE, YOU ARE YOUR OWN WORST ENEMY, YOU SAY THINGS ABOUT YOURSELF THAT YOU WOULD NEVER SAY ABOUT ANYONE ELSE. YOU MUST FIRST MAKE PEACE WITH YOURSELF AND PEACE WITH GOD. IF YOU PUT YOURSELF DOWN, THE SPIRIT OF DEATH MOVES ON YOUR WORDS, NOW CANCEL YOUR OWN WORDS, CONFESS, REPENT, TAKE COMMUNION AND SPEAK YOUR TESTIMONY, I AM A SON OF GOD, THIS IS THE TRUTH AND THE HOLY SPIRIT MOVES ON YOUR WORDS, AND MANIFESTS THEM IN YOUR LIFE. THIS MANIFESTS IN LOVE, PEACE AND JOY WITH YOURSELF, WITH YOUR FAMILY, AND EVERYONE AROUND YOU, AND MOST IMPORTANTLY WITH GOD, JESUS CHRIST THE PRINCE OF ALL PEACE.

GOD'S SPIRITUAL CALL TO ACTION!

- A) SHARE MY LOVE, ETERNAL LIFE.
- B) BRING THEM INTO MY PRESENCE
- C) GET OUT OF THE WAY
- D) SET MY PEOPLE FREE, SET MY PEOPLE FREE, SET MY PEOPLE FREE

THE QUESTION: DO YOU LOVE THEM ENOUGH TO GIVE THEM THE TRUTH? ONLY THE REVOLUTIONARY TRUTH OF JESUS CHRIST WILL SET MY PEOPLE FREE.   YES!

GOD NEVER CHANGES!

GET A HOLD ON THIS ONE REVELATION, THIS DEEP TRUTH, AND YOUR LIFE WILL NEVER BE THE SAME. GOD CREATED EVERYTHING, NOTHING WAS CREATED THAT HE DID NOT CREATE, GOD'S TRUTH IS FOREVER, AND GOD NEVER CHANGES. GOD CREATED YOU IN HIS OWN IMAGE, AND GOD WILL ALWAYS LOVE YOU, HIS LOVE NEVER FAILS. GEN 2 GOD'S AMAZING GRACE, HIS UNLIMITED LOVE, IS FOREVER. EVERYBODY, INCLUDING YOU, IS IN HIS FAMILY TO START WITH UNTIL THE AGE OF CHOICE. THEN YOU CHOOSE LIFE OR DEATH. KNOW THIS, THIS IS HIS AMAZING GRACE, GOD WILL ALWAYS RECEIVE YOU BACK INTO HIS FAMILY, REGARDLESS OF WHO YOU ARE, CHRISTIAN, MUSLIM, HINDU, BUDHIST, ATHEIST, ETC. AND ALSO REGARDLESS OF WHAT YOU HAVE DONE. ALL YOU HAVE TO DO IS CHOOSE JESUS CHRIST, HE CHOSE YOU, CONFESS AND REPENT OF YOUR SIN (AGREEMENT WITH THE SPIRIT OF DEATH), BE BAPTIZED (HIS BLOOD WASHES AWAY ALL YOUR SIN (AGREEMENT WITH THE SPIRIT OF DEATH), AND ASK JESUS CHRIST TO FILL YOU WITH HIMSELF, (THE SPIRIT OF LIFE), TO EMPOWER YOU, TO SET YOU FREE TO BE ONE WITH HIM IN ETERNAL LIFE. THE POWER OF LIFE AND DEATH IS IN YOUR TONGUE, SPEAK LIFE NOT DEATH, CHOOSE LIFE NOT DEATH. NOW DAILY CONFESS AND REPENT OF YOUR SIN (AGREEMENT WITH THE SPIRIT OF DEATH), TAKE COMMUNION AND WASH AWAY ALL YOUR SIN (AGREEMENT WITH THE SPIRIT OF DEATH) AND ASK JESUS CHRIST TO FILL YOU WITH THE SPIRIT OF LIFE, TO SET YOU FREE, AND STAY SET FREE, TO BE ONE WITH

HIM IN ETERNAL LIFE. JESUS CHRIST IS THE SAME YESTERDAY, TODAY, AND FOREVER. HE SAYS WHAT HE MEANS AND HE MEANS WHAT HE SAYS. HE IS DOING TODAY WHAT HE DID YESTERDAY AND HE WILL DO IT FOREVER. EVERYTHING GOD PUT IN PLACE IS FOR YOUR GOOD. GOD PUT INTO PLACE HIS SUPERNATURAL AND NATURAL ORDER FOR ALL OF MANKIND TO FOLLOW. GOD PUT IN PLACE HIS PLAN FOR FORGIVENESS, SALVATION, HEALING, DELIVERANCE, RESTORATION, AND EMPOWERMENT OF HIS TRUE SONS AND DAUGHTERS WITH HIMSELF, TO FOLLOW IN HIS FOOTSTEPS TO DESTROY THE WORKS OF THE DEVIL AND SET ALL MANKIND FREE TO ETERNAL LIFE, ETERNAL LIFE ON EARTH AS IT IS IN HEAVEN. GOD DID NOT CREATE GUILT, SHAME UNFORGIVENESS, BITTERNESS, ANGER, ANXIETY, FEAR, PRIDE, STRESS, RACISM, HATE, BIGOTRY, AND ANY AND ALL SICKNESS. THESE ARE ALL LIES OF THE DEVIL, SPIRIT OF DEATH, THAT YOU DO NOT WANT TO AGREE WITH. REALIZE, WHATEVER SPIRIT YOU AGREE WITH WILL MANIFEST IN YOUR LIFE, IF YOU AGREE AND BELIEVE WHAT THAT SPIRIT IS SAYING TO YOU. THE SPIRIT OF LIFE, THE HOLY SPIRIT WILL MANIFEST LIFE IN YOU. THIS IS TRUTH. THE SPIRIT OF DEATH WILL MANIFEST DEATH IN YOU. THE SPIRIT OF DEATH LIES TO YOU AND MANIPULATES (USES WITCHCRAFT), ON YOU TO GET YOU TO BELIEVE YOU ARE SICK. THE DOCTOR NAMES IT AND YOU AGREE AND BELIEVE IT. NOW, TO YOU IT IS REAL. IT IS NOT REAL, IT IS A LIE, GOD DID NOT CREATE IT. SICKNESS, DEATH, AND PAIN MANIFESTS IN YOUR BODY BECAUSE YOU AGREE AND BELIEVE IT. NOW, YOU CAN HURT YOURSELF, CAR WRECKS, POISON, ETC., STAY IN AGREEMENT WITH THE SPIRIT OF LIFE AND YOU WILL RESTORE QUICKLY. ALWAYS REMEMBER, YOU ARE EITHER IN AGREEMENT WITH GOD OR YOU ARE IN AGREEMENT WITH THE DEVIL. THE DEVIL IS DEATH, STEAL, KILL, AND DESTROY. GOD IS LIFE, LOVE, PEACE, AND JOY. HOW DID GOD HANDLE THIS, GOD SENT HIS ONLY BEGOTTEN SON, JESUS CHRIST, FROM HEAVEN TO EARTH, AND WHOSOEVER BELIEVES IN HIM AND FOLLOWS HIS

16

COMMANDMENTS (LOVE GOD, AND LOVE ONE ANOTHER AS I HAVE LOVED YOU) WILL NEVER DIE. YOU WILL HAVE ETERNAL LIFE ON EARTH AS IT IS IN HEAVEN, FOREVER IN JESUS CHRIST, CHOOSE LIFE NOT DEATH. JN 3

GOD HAS ALREADY REVEALED TO ME THAT THERE IS ONLY ONE ACCUSER – THE DEVIL – THE SPIRIT OF DEATH. WHEN YOU ACCUSE ANYONE OF ANYTHING, YOU GET INTO AN AGREEMENT WITH THE DEVIL – THE SPIRIT OF DEATH.

WHEN YOU ACCUSE, THE WORDS YOU USE, THE DEVIL HAS THE LEGAL RIGHT TO USE YOUR WORDS BACK ON YOU. MATT 7.

NOW, THE NEW REVELATION – I HAVE BEEN MINISTERING TO PEOPLE EXPLAINING THAT YOU ARE YOUR OWN WORST ENEMY. YOU WILL SAY THINGS ABOUT YOURSELF THAT YOU WOULD NEVER SAY TO SOMEONE ELSE. YOU ACTUALLY THINK THAT YOU CAN SAY THINGS ABOUT YOURSELF AND THAT IS OK....IT IS NOT. WHEN YOU ACCUSE YOURSELF YOU ARE ACTUALLY CREATING AN AGREEMENT WITH THE SPIRIT OF DEATH. THAT IS WHY YOU MUST CONFESS AND REPENT, TAKE YOUR COMMUNION, AND SPEAK YOUR TESTIMONY TO BE FREE.

MIGHTY REVELATION....

I WAS MINISTERING TO AN 82 YEAR OLD MAN AND GOD REVEALED THAT YOU CANNOT LOVE GOD UNTIL YOU LOVE YOURSELF BECAUSE YOU ARE MADE IN HIS IMAGE – FULL CIRCLE.

MATTHEW 22 – JESUS SAID THOU SHALT LOVE THE LORD THY GOD WITH ALL THY HEART AND WITH ALL THY SOUL AND WITH ALL THY MIND. THIS IS THE FIRST AND GREAT COMMANDMENT. THE SECOND IS LIKE UNTO IT, THOU SHALT LOVE YOUR NEIGHBOR AS THYSELF.

MY QUESTION...HOW MANY OF YOU LOVE YOURSELF? THIS GOES HAND-IN-HAND WITH WHAT WE HAVE BEEN TALKING ABOUT. WE HAVE PLACED FAR MORE EMPHASIS ON THE PART OF NEIGHBOR THAN MYSELF. THIS AGAIN IS THE SPIRIT OF DEATH THAT HAS BEEN HANDED DOWN THROUGH THE GENERATIONS. WE HAVE BEEN TAUGHT NOT TO LOVE OURSELVES. HOW MANY TIMES HAVE YOU HEARD...OH YOU THINK YOUR SOMETHING....YOU THINK YOU'RE BETTER THAN SOMEONE ELSE....WHY DO YOU THINK SO MUCH OF YOURSELF.....OR WHY DO YOU THINK YOU'RE SO SPECIAL? AND ON IT GOES. WE HAVE BEEN TAUGHT THE SPIRIT OF DEATH INSTEAD OF LIFE. HOW CAN YOU LOVE YOUR NEIGHBOR, MUSLIM, HINDU, ATHEIST, OTHER CHRISTIANS, IF YOU DO NOT FIRST LOVE GOD, THEN YOURSELF, IT IS IMPOSSIBLE.

YOU MUST FIRST LOVE GOD, THEN YOURSELF AND YOUR NEIGHBOR SEES THE LOVE OF JESUS CHRIST IN YOU. THE ONLY WAY YOU CAN EVER LOVE YOURSELF IS TO BE SET FREE FROM YOUR SIN, BE FILLED WITH JESUS CHRIST REALIZE WHO YOU ARE...YOU ARE MADE IN THE IMAGE OF GOD. GOD IS ALL IN ALL, HE IS THE CREATOR OF ALL LIFE. WE ARE ALL MADE IN HIS IMAGE. SOME OF US ARE MADE IN THE MALE IMAGE AND SOME IN THE FEMALE IMAGE. ONE IS JUST AS IMPORTANT AS THE OTHER, IT

TAKES BOTH MALE AND FEMALE TO CREATE LIFE. MAN WITH MAN, OR WOMAN WITH WOMAN LEADS TO DEATH. HERE IS ANOTHER LIE OF THE DEVIL EXPOSED, YOU ARE NOT A MALE AND YOU ARE NOT A FEMALE, YOU ARE YOU. THIS LEADS TO CONFUSION, GOD IS NOT A GOD OF CONFUSION. REMEMBER ANY TYPE OF MANIPULATION SUCH AS CONFUSION IS WITCHCRAFT, DO NOT FALL FOR IT. GOD MAKES IT VERY CLEAR ABOUT HOMOSEXUALITY AND PERVERSION, THIS IS SIN, STAY AWAY FROM IT. THE DEVIL WOULD TRY AND TRICK YOU, AND GET YOU TO BELIEVE, IF YOU DON'T KNOW WHICH SEX YOU ARE WHAT DIFFERENCE DOES IT MAKE. DO NOT BELIEVE THE HYPE AND THE LIES OF THE MEDIA, THIS IS THE SPIRIT OF DEATH AT WORK. IF YOU DON'T KNOW WHO YOU ARE THEN THE DEVIL CAN CONTROL YOU. IF YOU KNOW WHO YOU ARE, YOU CANNOT BE CONTROLLED, YOU ARE FREE AND YOU CAN HELP OTHERS BE SET FREE. THIS IS WHO YOU ARE AND NEVER FORGET IT.

YOU ARE A TRUE SON OR DAUGHTER OF GOD, MADE IN THE IMAGE OF GOD, LOVED, ACCEPTED, AND RESTORED WITH ETERNAL LIFE ON EARTH AS IT IS IN HEAVEN. JESUS TOOK IT ONE STEP FURTHER...."LOVE ONE ANOTHER AS I HAVE LOVED YOU!" JESUS LOVES EVERYONE THE SAME AND JESUS NEVER CHANGES. HE MADE A WAY WHERE THERE WAS NO WAY TO BECOME TRUE SONS AND DAUGHTERS OF GOD, TO RECEIVE ETERNAL LIFE AND TO SPREAD THE GOOD NEWS....THAT ETERNAL LIFE IS HERE AND NOW, AVAILABLE TO ALL MANKIND, THROUGH HIM.

LOVE, PEACE AND JOY, QUIT STRIVING AND RECEIVE!

REMEMBER AS A TRUE SON AND DAUGHTER OF GOD YOU HAVE THE POWER AND KNOWLEDGE OF THE HOLY GHOST TO HELP YOUR NEIGHBOR HAVE WHAT YOU HAVE AND THEN YOU WILL HAVE MORE THAN A NEIGHBOR, BUT A TRUE BROTHER OR SISTER IN CHRIST WITH ETERNAL LIFE WHO CAN TAKE FORTH THE MESSAGE AND HELP OTHERS TO JOIN IN THE FAMILY....THE FAMILY OF GOD WORLDWIDE!

NOW ALL OF THIS CAN HELP YOU UNDERSTAND REV 12 "AND THEY OVERCAME HIM (THE SPIRIT OF DEATH) BY THE <u>BLOOD OF THE LAMB</u> AND BY THE WORD OF THEIR <u>TESTIMONY</u> "

YOUR TESTIMONY: I AM A TRUE SON OR DAUGHTER OF GOD, MADE IN THE IMAGE OF GOD, LOVED, ACCEPTED, AND RESTORED WITH ETERNAL LIFE. "FOR THE WAGES OF SIN (AGREEMENT WITH THE SPIRIT OF DEATH) IS DEATH, BUT THE GIFT OF GOD IS ETERNAL LIFE THROUGH JESUS CHRIST OUR LORD" ROMAN 7.

HOLY SPIRIT, HELP US GRASP THE FACT THAT IN ETERNAL LIFE THERE IS NO SICKNESS, NO DISEASE, NO PAIN, NO SUFFERING, AND NO AGING. THAT WE HAVE AUTHORITY OVER DEATH AND ALL SYMPTOMS RELATED TO AND MANIFESTING DEATH. THERE IS RESTORATION AND RECREATION, RESTORATION OF ALL IN ALL AS IF IT NEVER HAPPENED. ETERNAL LIFE ON EARTH AS IT IS IN HEAVEN.

JESUS CHRIST THE ROCK!

JESUS CHRIST IS THE LIVING SON OF GOD (YAHWEH). JESUS CHRIST IS GOD (YAHWEH). JESUS CHRIST IS THE HOLY LIVING WORD OF GOD. JESUS CHRIST IS LIFE, LIFE MORE ABUNDANTLY, ETERNAL LIFE, THAT IS WHY HE CAN GIVE IT TO YOU, WHEN YOU BECOME ONE WITH HIM. JESUS CHRIST IS THE ROCK, THE FOUNDATION OF ALL CHRISTIANITY AND ALL OF CREATION. JESUS CHRIST IS ABSOLUTE POWER AND AUTHORITY AND IS IN TOTAL CONTROL OF ALL CREATION. JESUS CHRIST IS THE SAME YESTERDAY, TODAY AND FOREVER. JESUS CHRIST IS HEAD OF HIS CHURCH, AND ONLY THE TRUTH OF JESUS CHRIST CAN SET YOU FREE AND THIS MUST NEVER BE COMPROMISED. REALIZE, YOU ARE EITHER IN AGREEMENT WITH JESUS CHRIST OR YOU ARE IN AGREEMENT WITH THE ANTI-CHRIST. YOU EITHER HAVE THE DNA (SPIRIT OF LIFE) OF JESUS CHRIST OR THE DNA (SPIRIT OF DEATH) OF THE ANTI-CHRIST. THINK LONG AND HARD ABOUT THIS REVOLUTIONARY TRUTH, WHO ARE YOU IN AGREEMENT WITH AND WHO'S DNA DO YOU CARRY? ARE YOU IN AGREEMENT WITH THE SPIRIT OF LIFE OR ARE YOU IN AGREEMENT WITH THE SPIRIT OF DEATH? JESUS CHRIST IS LIFE, ETERNAL LIFE, THE ANTI-CHRIST IS DEATH, ETERNAL DEATH, CHOOSE LIFE NOT DEATH, SPEAK LIFE NOT DEATH, LIVE IN PEACE LOVE AND JOY AND SHARE YOUR SMILE.

THE SECRET!

" THE SECRET TO THE MYSTERY OF THE GOSPEL IS FOR YOU TO LOVE AND ACCEPT JESUS CHRIST AS HE LOVES AND ACCEPTS YOU AND YOU WILL HAVE ETERNAL LIFE" THS (THE HOLY SPIRIT) "JESUS CHRIST (ETERNAL LIFE) CAME IN THE FLESH TO RESTORE THE ETERNAL LIFE COVENANT, INTIMACY (LOVE AND ACCEPTANCE) BETWEEN GOD (ETERNAL LIFE) AND MAN." THS

REALIZE, EVERYONE'S MOST SECRETIVE, DEEPEST, INNERMOST DESIRE IS TO BE LOVED AND ACCEPTED!

JESUS CHRIST, AMAZING GRACE AND LOVE, PROCLAIMS "YOU WILL KNOW MY PEOPLE BY THEIR LOVE,"JN13 AND MY "LOVE NEVER FAILS."1STCOR13 THIS AMAZING LOVE IS JESUS CHRIST (SPIRIT OF LIFE) IN YOU, SHINING FORTH PEACE AND JOY. "I GIVE YOU MY PEACE, NOT AS THE WORLD GIVETH IT, BUT MY PEACE."JN 14. THE PEACE THAT PASSES ALL UNDERSTANDING. PHIL 14 THIS PEACE COMES FROM KNOWING THAT JESUS CHRIST SITS ON THE THRONE, HE IS IN TOTAL CONTROL, ALL THINGS ARE POSSIBLE WITH GOD, AND GOD HAS ALL POWER AND ALL AUTHORITY. JESUS CHRIST HAS GIVEN YOU HIS POWER AND AUTHORITY OVER THE DEVIL AND ALL OF HIS DEMONS. LUKE 10. "THE WICKED ONE CAN TOUCH YOU NOT."1STJN 5 YOUR JOY SPRINGS FORTH IN KNOWING THAT IN BECOMING ONE WITH JESUS CHRIST, YOU ARE IN THE FAMILY OF GOD, YOU HAVE HIS DNA, (SPIRIT OF LIFE), YOU HAVE ACHIEVED YOUR GREATEST DESIRE OF LOVE AND ACCEPTANCE, YOU HAVE THE VICTORY OF ETERNAL LIFE ON EARTH AS IT IS IN HEAVEN, 1STJN5, YOU HAVE BEEN TRANSLATED OUT OF DARKNESS INTO HIS MARVELOUS LIGHT,1STPETER2, AND NOW JESUS CHRIST CAN USE YOU TO

SHINE FORTH HIS LIGHT INTO THE WORLD AND HELP SET ALL
MANKIND FREE TO ETERNAL LIFE. THE JOY OF GOD, IN YOU, IS
YOUR STRENGTH," FOR GREATER IS HE THAT IS IN YOU, THAN HE
THAT IS IN THE WORLD. "THE SPIRIT OF LIFE IN YOU OVERCOMES
THE SPIRIT OF DEATH.

JESUS CHRIST REVOLUTIONARY!

JESUS CHRIST CAME IN THE FLESH, HIS LOVE IS UNFATHOMABLE
AND HIS MERCY ENDURETH FOREVER. JESUS CHRIST PREACHED
CONFESS AND REPENT OF YOUR SIN (AGREEMENT WITH THE
DEVIL, THE SPIRIT OF DEATH), BECOME ONE WITH ME AND I WILL
GIVE YOU REST, ETERNAL LIFE ON EARTH AS IT IS IN HEAVEN.
JESUS CHRIST SET AT LIBERTY AND HEALED EVERYONE THAT
CAME TO HIM, MIRACLES ABOUNDED, HE TURNED THE WORLD
UPSIDE DOWN AND MADE IT POSSIBLE FOR ALL OF HIS CREATION
TO COME TO ETERNAL LIFE. NOW, AS TRUE SONS AND
DAUGHTERS OF YAHWEH WE ARE TO FOLLOW IN THE FOOTSTEPS
OF JESUS CHRIST, SHARE HIS LOVE AND WITH HIM DO THE SAME
MIRACLES. WE WILL DISCUSS THIS IN DETAIL AND VISIT WITH
MEN AND WOMEN , THE YOUNG AND THE OLD WHO HAVE BEEN
RESTORED, CANCER GONE, RAISED FROM THE DEAD, AND ALL
OPPRESSION OF THE DEVIL (SPIRIT OF DEATH) DESTROYED,
DEPRESSION (SPIRIT OF DEATH) GONE.

"I AM COMING!"

JESUS CHRIST MAKES IT VERY CLEAR, HE WILL RETURN WHEN HIS
PEOPLE START PROCLAIMING "BLESSED IS HE WHO COMES IN THE

23

NAME OF YAHWEH". MAT 23 HALLELUJAH! COME ON CHURCH, THIS IS PART OF OUR SPIRITUAL CALL TO ACTION TO USHER IN THE COMING OF JESUS CHRIST. PREACH THE TRUE GOSPEL OF THE KINGDOM, MATT 24. REMEMBER, GOD CREATED TIME FOR US TO LIVE IN UNTIL WE BECOME ONE WITH HIM. THERE IS NO TIME WITH GOD, IT IS ALWAYS NOW. GOD CREATED EVERYTHING AND HAS FULL ABSOLUTE POWER AND AUTHORITY OVER HIS CREATION. HIS CREATION DOES NOT HAVE POWER AND AUTHORITY OVER THE CREATOR. **WHEN WE BECOME ONE WITH JESUS CHRIST, FILLED WITH THE HOLY SPIRIT, HE GIVES US HIS POWER AND AUTHORITY TO USE HIS NAME, (POWER OF ATTORNEY), OVER CREATION. REMEMBER, GOD CREATED THE ANGEL WHO BECAME THE DEVIL, THE SPIRIT OF THE DEATH. WHEN WE BECOME ONE WITH JESUS CHRIST, THE CREATOR OF EVERYTHING, WE HAVE POWER AND AUTHORITY OVER THE DEVIL, THE SPIRIT OF DEATH AND OVER THE NATURAL REALM THAT HE, JESUS CHRIST, CREATED!** JESUS CHRIST WILL LEAVE THE SUPERNATURAL NOW AND COME INTO OUR NATURAL TIME THAT HE CREATED TO ACCOMPLISH HIS FULFILLMENT OF HIS PURPOSE TO SET ALL OF MANKIND FREE TO ETERNAL LIFE AND DESTROY THE WORKS OF THE DEVIL AND HIS ANTI-CHRIST.

THE TRUE NAME OF GOD!

THE NAME GOD AND LORD ARE GENERIC TERMS. THE TRUE BIBLICAL NAME OF FATHER GOD IS YAHWEH, HIS SON IS JESUS CHRIST (YESHUA – ANOINTED ONE), AND THE HOLY SPIRIT (RUACH HA KODESH – THE BREATH OF YAHWEH). ALL THREE ARE ONE IN THAT THEY ARE THE ONE TRUE CREATOR OF ALL CREATION, JESUS CHRIST AND THE HOLY SPIRIT CAME OUT OF THE FATHER'S BOSOM AND ALL THREE HAVE THE SAME DNA, SPIRIT OF LIFE, ETERNAL LIFE. JOHN 1.

THE MOST IMPORTANT REVELATION FOR ALL OF CREATION!

THIS IS THE MOST IMPORTANT PART OF THE REVOLUTION, WHY JESUS CHRIST TRULY CAME, AND WHO YOU CAN BE BECAUSE OF HIS COMING, THE TRUE GOSPEL MESSAGE OF THE KINGDOM. JESUS CHRIST PROCLAIMED "AND THIS GOSPEL OF THE KINGDOM SHALL BE PREACHED IN ALL THE WORLD FOR A WITNESS UNTO ALL NATIONS, AND THEN SHALL THE END COME." MAT 24

FATHER YAHWEH HAS SENT US FORTH WITH HIS LIVING WATER, SPIRIT FILLED WORDS OF ETERNAL LIFE, FOR HIS RESTORATION OF SPIRIT, SOUL, AND BODY, FOR ALL MANKIND. FATHER YAHWEH, THE GREAT I AM IS TOTALLY SUPREME. REALIZE, THERE IS ONLY ONE GOD, FATHER YAHWEH, HIS SON JESUS CHRIST, AND HIS HOLY SPIRIT, AND THEY ARE ALL POWER AND AUTHORITY, ETERNAL LIFE ON EARTH AS IT IS IN HEAVEN. THE DEVIL AND ALL HIS MINIONS, DEMONS, ARE TOTALLY DEFEATED, SIN IS DEFEATED, SICKNESS IS DEFEATED, AND DEATH DEFEATED.

HE CAME: JESUS CHRIST, SON OF YAHWEH, LEFT HEAVEN AND CAME TO EARTH, IN THE FLESH, AS A BABY BOY. HE CAME CARRYING YAHWEH'S DNA, SPIRIT OF ETERNAL LIFE, PEACE ON EARTH, GOODWILL TOWARD MEN –

HE BLED: FOR REMISSION OF ALL OUR SINS, OH HAPPY DAY WHEN JESUS WASHED ALL MY SIN (AGREEMENT WITH THE SPIRIT OF DEATH) AWAY –

HE DIED: ON THE CROSS, RATIFYING THE ETERNAL LIFE COVENANT, HE SAID "IT IS FINISHED", HE WAS TALKING ABOUT THE NEW ETERNAL LIFE COVENANT–

HE AROSE: VICTORY OVER DEATH, ETERNAL LIFE OVERCOMES ETERNAL DEATH, THE LAST THING TO OVERCOME WAS SPIRIT OF DEATH, HE TOOK THE SPIRIT OF DEATH CAPTIVE –

HE ASCENDED: BACK INTO HEAVEN, SEATED AT THE RIGHT HAND OF YAHWEH, I AM, AND HE IS ON OUR SIDE, AND MEDIATES, INTERCEDES FOR US WITH YAHWEH.

THE ANSWER: JESUS CHRIST, ETERNAL LIFE, ENDURED ALL OF THIS TORMENT FOR ONE PURPOSE, TO MAKE IT POSSIBLE FOR YOU TO BE BLESSED BY THE COMING OF YAHWEH, THE HOLY SPIRIT, THE SPIRIT OF ETERNAL LIFE, THE SPIRIT OF JESUS CHRIST TO LIVE INSIDE YOU, MAKING YOUR BODY HIS HOME, HIS SANCTUARY, HIS HOLY CHURCH. HIS HOLINESS IS NOW YOUR HOLINESS. THUS EMPOWERING TRUE SONS AND DAUGHTERS OF YAHWEH, WITH YAHWEH'S HOLY SPIRIT POWER AND FIRE AND YAHWEH'S DNA, (SPIRIT OF ETERNAL LIFE) TO MANIFEST HIS HOLY RIGHTEOUSNESS, TO TAKE HIS PLACE ON THIS EARTH, SPEAKING AND ACTING ON HIS LIVING SPIRIT WORDS OF TRUTH AND LOVE, DESTROYING THE WORKS OF THE DEVIL, RESTORATION OF ALL IN ALL, ABOUNDING IN MIRACLES OF SPIRIT, SOUL, AND BODY, SETTING ALL MANKIND FREE TO ETERNAL LIFE, TRUE EMISSARIES OF JESUS CHRIST.

THE MYSTERY OF THE HOLY SPIRIT BAPTISM!

"BLESSED ARE THEY WHICH DO HUNGER AND THIRST AFTER RIGHTEOUSNESS, FOR THEY SHALL BE FILLED." MAT 5 " IF YE THEN, BEING EVIL, KNOW HOW TO GIVE GOOD GIFTS UNTO YOU CHILDREN, HOW MUCH MORE SHALL YOUR HEAVENLY FATHER GIVE THE HOLY SPIRIT TO THEM THAT ASK HIM."LUKE 11. JESUS CHRIST PAID THE PRICE AND YOU HAVE RECEIVED HIM AS YOUR LORD AND SAVIOUR, AND NOW YOU HUNGER AND THIRST FOR THE DEEP MYSTERIES OF GOD, AND YOUR GREATEST DESIRE

IS TO BE MORE LIKE HIM AND HAVE HIM SPEAK AND WORK HIS MIRACLES THROUGH YOU. HERE IS GOD'S HOLY ANSWER, FIRST YOU CONFESS AND REPENT OF YOUR SIN (AGREEMENT WITH THE SPIRIT OF DEATH, TAKE COMMUNION, WASHING AWAY THE SPIRIT OF DEATH, SETTING YOU FREE, AND NOW YOU ASK JESUS CHRIST TO BAPTIZE YOU WITH HIS HOLY SPIRIT. THE HOLY SPIRIT NOW FLOWS FROM THE SOUL, (MIND, WILL, AND EMOTIONS), OF JESUS CHRIST INTO YOUR SOUL, (MIND, WILL, AND EMOTIONS, AND INTO YOUR SPIRIT. YOUR SPIRIT IS NOW AWAKENED BY THE SPIRIT OF ETERNAL LIFE AND THE HOLY SPIRIT IS FREE TO SPEAK THROUGH YOU THE LANGUAGE OF JESUS CHRIST, THE LANGUAGE AND FREQUENCY OF ETERNAL LIFE, THE LANGUAGE AND FREQUENCY OF CREATION. NOW, ASK HIM TO SPEAK THROUGH YOU THE MYSTERIES OF GOD. THIS IS FAR ABOVE ANOINTING, THIS IS TOTAL BAPTISM OF YOUR SOUL AND SPIRIT INTO THE SOUL AND SPIRIT OF JESUS CHRIST, AND HIS SOUL AND SPIRIT INTO YOURS. YOU NOW HAVE THE MIND AND HEART OF JESUS CHRIST. YOU ARE NOW EMPOWERED BY THE SPIRIT OF ETERNAL LIFE TO TAKE HIS PLACE, AND WITH HIM AND THROUGH HIM TO SPEAK HIS LANGUAGE, TO BROADCAST THE FREQUENCY OF JESUS CHRIST, PERFORM HIS MIRACLES, DESTROY THE WORKS OF THE DEVIL AND SET ALL OF MANKIND AND ALL OF CREATION FREE TO ETERNAL LIFE IN HIM.

THE HOLY SPIRIT!

THE HOLY SPIRIT, THE SPIRIT OF HOLINESS, IS GENTLE AND PEACEFUL AND WILL NEVER FORCE YOU TO DO ANYTHING THAT YOU ARE UNCOMFORTABLE WITH. BUT HE IS ALSO YAHWEH, THE HOLY SPIRIT, BREATH OF LIFE, GIVER OF LIFE, EVERY WHERE HE GOES HE BRINGS (RESTORES) LIFE AND IF YOU WILL ALLOW HIM, HE WILL USE YOU, TO USE A MILITARY TERM, A COMMAND BASE OF OPERATIONS TO WORK FROM AND THROUGH TO DESTROY

THE WORKS (SPIRIT OF DEATH) OF THE DEVIL. AND WITH YOUR PERMISSION AND ENTHUSIASM, YOU ARE NOW A SOLDIER IN JESUS CHRIST'S ARMY TO USE TO BRING FORTH HIS OBJECTIVE, LIFE AND LIFE MORE ABUNDANTLY, ETERNAL LIFE FOR ALL MANKIND ON EARTH AS IT IS IN HEAVEN. YOU ARE NOW A TRUE EMISSARY OF JESUS CHRIST.

JESUS CHRIST RETURNS!

JESUS CHRIST PROCLAIMED: "I AM COMING.... I AM THE RESURRECTION AND THE LIFE, THOSE WHO BELIEVE IN ME SHALL NEVER DIE, TO KNOW ME IS ETERNAL LIFE. JESUS CHRIST IS COMING BACK TO TAKE HIS FAMILY HOME TO HEAVEN, ETERNAL LIFE. THEN, JESUS CHRIST IS COMING AS THE GREAT "I AM", WITH HIS SAINTS, DESTROYING THE ANTI-CHRIST, AND ALL THE WORKS OF THE DEVIL, SPIRIT OF DEATH, SETTING ALL MANKIND FREE TO RULE AND REIGN FOR A 1000 YEARS. THE CHOICE IS NOW YOURS, TO BELIEVE AND RECEIVE WHAT JESUS CHRIST HAS PREPARED FOR YOU.... CHOOSE LIFE NOT DEATH!

BELIEVE & RECEIVE!

EVERYTHING ABOUT CHRISTIANITY IS SUPERNATURAL!

THE REVOLUTIONARY TRUTH OF YAHWEH IS EVERYTHING IS ABOUT LIFE, LIFE MORE ABUNDANTLY, ETERNAL LIFE. JESUS CHRIST SAID "GO MAKE DISCIPLES", BAPTIZING THEM IN THE NAME OF THE FATHER GOD, AND OF THE SON, JESUS CHRIST, AND OF THE HOLY GHOST. MAT.28 DISCIPLES WITH THE SPIRIT OF ETERNAL LIFE, ENDUED WITH HOLY SPIRIT POWER, TO STAND UP, SPEAK THE TRUTH IN LOVE, ACT ON THE TRUTH,   DESTROY THE WORKS OF THE DEVIL, (A CREATED BEING), THE SPIRIT OF DEATH,

TAKE THE WORLD BACK, SET MANKIND FREE, NO LONGER VICTIMS AND SLAVES, BUT NOW ETERNAL LIFE OVERCOMERS. REALIZE THE ENEMY IS THE DEVIL, SPIRIT OF DEATH, SPIRITUAL WICKEDNESS IN HIGH PLACES, NOT FLESH AND BLOOD, NOT YOUR FELLOW MEMBERS OF MANKIND. EPH 6. NOW, REALIZE THE DEVIL AND DEATH ARE TOTALLY DEFEATED. THE DEVIL HAS NO POWER OR AUTHORITY, ALL HE CAN DO IS LIE AND TRY TO GET YOU TO AGREE WITH HIS LIES. JESUS CHRIST BOLDLY PROCLAIMED, ALL POWER IS GIVEN UNTO ME IN HEAVEN AND IN EARTH. MAT.28. FEAR NOT, I AM THE FIRST AND THE LAST. I AM HE THAT LIVETH, AND WAS DEAD AND BEHOLD, I AM ALIVE FOR EVERMORE, AMEN, AND I HAVE THE KEYS OF HELL AND DEATH. REV.1 JESUS CHRIST IS READY FOR HIS ARMY TO ARISE IN HIS POWER OF LOVE AND ACCEPTANCE, AND TAKE BACK WHAT HE GAVE US. YAHWEH GAVE ADAM HIS KNOWLEDGE AND HIS NATURE, HIS DNA, SPIRIT OF ETERNAL LIFE. THE DEVIL STOLE FROM ADAM YAHWEH'S KNOWLEDGE AND YAHWEH'S DNA. THE DEVIL REPLACED IN ADAM THE KNOWLEDGE OF GOOD AND EVIL AND HIS DNA, SPIRIT OF DEATH. MANKIND HAS NOW FALLEN AND CARRIES THE DEVIL'S DNA, THE SPIRIT OF DEATH. JESUS CHRIST CAME AND DESTROYED THE WORKS OF THE DEVIL AND TOOK IT ALL BACK. ONLY JESUS CHRIST CAN BAPTIZE AND BLESS YOU WITH THE HOLY SPIRIT AND HIS DNA, SPIRIT OF ETERNAL LIFE. WHEN YOU RECEIVE JESUS CHRIST AND TRULY BECOME ONE WITH HIM, YOU RECEIVE BACK HIS NATURE, HIS DNA, ETERNAL LIFE OF YAHWEH. THIS IS WHY WE ARE THE FAMILY OF YAHWEH, WE HAVE HIS DNA, SPIRIT OF ETERNAL LIFE. IN YAHWEH'S DNA, SPIRIT OF ETERNAL LIFE, THERE IS NO EVIL, NO SIN, NO SICKNESS, NO DEATH. THIS IS WHY OLD THINGS ARE PASSED AWAY AND ALL THINGS BECOME NEW. THIS IS WHY WE ARE A NEW CREATURE IN YAHWEH'S FAMILY, WE HAVE HIS NATURE, HIS DNA, SPIRIT OF ETERNAL LIFE, UNLIMITED LOVE, AUTHORITY OVER CREATION INCLUDING THE DEVIL, A CREATED BEING. WE ARE BORN AGAIN

29

IN HIS HOLY SPIRIT, HIS DNA, SPIRIT OF ETERNAL LIFE, TRUE SONS AND DAUGHTERS OF YAHWEH. REALIZE, EVERYTIME WE TAKE COMMUNION, WE TAKE IN A FRESH TRANSFUSION OF JESUS CHRIST'S DNA, HIS BODY AND BLOOD, THE SPIRIT OF ETERNAL LIFE. THIS FRESH TRANSFUSION OF JESUS CHRIST'S DNA, THE SPIRIT OF ETERNAL LIFE, DESTROYS THE OPPRESSION OF THE DEVIL, THE SPIRIT OF DEATH, DOWN TO THE CELLULAR LEVEL. I BELIEVE IT AND I RECEIVE IT AND I THANK JESUS CHRIST FOR IT.

COMMUNION – FREEDOM IN JESUS CHRIST!

REALIZE, THIS IS THE REASON THAT THE DEVIL HAS USED EVERY TRICK IN THE BOOK TO BLIND AND DECEIVE THE CHURCH TO THIS POWER AVAILABLE TO THEM. A LOT OF CHURCHES ARE BLINDED TO THE TRUTH OF COMMUNION AND ONLY HAVE IT ONCE EVERY FEW MONTHS. THIS POWER IS AVAILABLE TO YOU. YOU DO NOT NEED A PASTOR, PRIEST, ETC. TO ADMINISTER COMMUNION TO YOU. THIS IS BETWEEN **YOU AND JESUS CHRIST**. YOU SHOULD TAKE COMMUNION, THIS FRESH TRANSFUSION OF JESUS CHRIST'S DNA, SPIRIT OF ETERNAL LIFE, A MINIMUM OF ONCE A DAY. I PERSONALLY TAKE COMMUNION FOUR TIMES A DAY, BEFORE EVERY MEAL AND BEFORE I GO TO BED. I ALSO TAKE COMMUNION WITH EVERYONE I MINISTER TO. REMEMBER, NEVER TAKE COMMUNION UNTIL YOU HAVE CONFESSED AND REPENTED OF YOUR SIN. THIS YOU DO IN REMEMBRANCE OF JESUS CHRIST. THIS STOPS THE DEVIL COLD AND GETS HIM OFF OF YOUR SOUL, ALL OPPRESSION, SPIRIT OF DEATH, CEASES AND YOU ARE SET FREE. NOW, CONFESS, REPENT, AND TAKE COMMUNION OFTEN AND STAY SET FREE. YOU NOW HAVE THE ANSWER TO FREEDOM IN JESUS CHRIST. THE HOLY SPIRIT WILL NOW REVEAL TO YOU A MYSTERY. WHEN YOU HAVE CONFESSED AND REPENTED OF YOUR SIN, AND YOU ARE THEN BAPTIZED IN WATER, THIS WATER BECOMES THE BLOOD OF JESUS CHRIST IN

THE SPIRIT REALM AND WASHES AWAY ALL YOUR SIN, AGREEMENT WITH THE SPIRIT OF DEATH, NOW YOU ARE CLEAN. IF YOU WERE TO SIN AGAIN, YOU CONFESS, REPENT AND TAKE COMMUNION, THE BODY AND BLOOD OF JESUS CHRIST. THE SOLID FOOD YOU EAT BECOMES THE BODY OF JESUS CHRIST IN THE SPIRIT REALM. HE IS THE BREAD OF LIFE, ETERNAL LIFE. THIS BODY, HIS SKIN, MUST BE BROKEN, CUT, OPENED UP SO THAT HIS BLOOD CAN POUR OUT. THE LIQUID YOU DRINK BECOMES THE BLOOD OF JESUS CHRIST IN THE SPIRIT REALM AND AGAIN WASHES AWAY ALL YOUR SIN, AGREEMENT WITH THE SPIRIT OF DEATH, YOU ARE TOTALLY FREE AGAIN. YOU ARE NOW CLEANSED OF ALL UNRIGHTOUSNESS, SPIRITUALLY, SOULFULLY AND PHYSICALLY. HALLELUJAH!.... ETERNAL LIFE ON EARTH AS IT IS IN HEAVEN, LOVE, PEACE, AND JOY ARE NOW YOURS, SHARE THIS BLESSING WITH EVERYONE YOU MEET. JESUS CHRIST MADE A WAY WHERE THERE WAS NO WAY, AND WE NOW HAVE FREE WILL TO TAKE BACK WHAT HE GAVE US.

JESUS CHRIST'S PRAYER!

REMEMBER, JESUS CHRIST'S PRAYER "FATHER I WOULD THAT THEY WOULD BE ONE AS WE ARE ONE". HOW ARE FATHER YAHWEH AND JESUS CHRIST AND THE HOLY SPIRIT ONE? THEY ALL HAVE THE SAME DNA, SPIRIT OF ETERNAL LIFE. JESUS CHRIST WENT ON FURTHER TO SAY "AND THE GLORY WHICH THOU GAVEST ME I HAVE GIVEN THEM, THAT THEY MAY BE ONE, EVEN AS WE ARE ONE". THE GLORY IS THE DNA OF YAHWEH, SPIRIT OF ETERNAL LIFE. JN17. ALL THINGS ARE POSSIBLE WITH JESUS CHRIST, WE HAVE HIS DNA, SPIRIT OF ETERNAL LIFE AND HIS POWER OF ATTORNEY TO BRING IT FORTH. JESUS CHRIST IS THE SAME YESTERDAY, TODAY AND FOREVER. THERE IS NO DEATH

WITH JESUS CHRIST, LIFE OVERTHROWS DEATH, ETERNAL LIFE DESTROYS DEATH. JN10.

REBELLION – AGREEMENT WITH THE DEVIL!

NOW, I WANT YOU TO LISTEN VERY CLOSELY TO WHAT I AM ABOUT TO SAY TO YOU. THERE IS A NATURAL ORDER OF GOD, THAT HE ESTABLISHED FOR ALL MANKIND. REBELLION AGAINST GOD'S NATURAL ORDER IS SIN, AGREEMENT WITH THE SPIRIT OF DEATH, AND OPENS THE DOOR FOR THE DEVIL TO COME IN. THIS STARTED IN THE GARDEN OF EDEN. ADAM'S REBELLION, THE FIRST SIN, IS THE FIRST AGREEMENT WITH THE SPIRIT OF DEATH.

REBELLION – ABORTION – BLOOD SACRIFICE!

TWO DAYS AFTER THE HOLY SPIRIT GAVE ME THE REVELATION OF DNA, HE AGAIN SPOKE TO ME THESE WORDS " IT IS IMPOSSIBLE FOR YOU TO HAVE MY DNA, SPIRIT OF LIFE, AND THINK THAT THE MURDER AND THE SACRIFICE OF THE INNOCENT IS ACCEPTABLE." THE INSTANT THE BABY IS CONCEIVED, GOD BREATHES LIFE INTO THE BABY, HE BREATHES HIS SPIRIT INTO THE CHILD. THIS CHILD IS NOW ALIVE AND HAS A DIFFERENT DNA THAN THE MOTHER OR THE FATHER. THIS CHILD NOW HAS ITS OWN DNA, A COMBINATION OF THE TWO. THE MOTHER IS NOW THE HOST FOR A LIVING BEING, WHICH HAS A DIFFERENT DNA THAN HERS LIVING INSIDE HER UNTIL TIME OF BIRTH. SHE HAS BEEN BLESSED BY GOD TO NURTURE AND BRING NEW LIFE INTO THIS WORLD AND THE OPPORTUNITY TO UNDERSTAND AND EXPERIENCE WHAT TRUE LOVE IS ALL ABOUT. IF SHE HAS AN ABORTION, SHE MISSES OUT ON ONE OF GOD'S GREATEST BLESSINGS, AND THEN HAS TO DEAL WITH THE SPIRIT OF DEATH. MY GRANDSONS WIFE, BROUGHT TEARS TO MY EYES AFTER HER SON WAS BORN, WHEN SHE SAID "I DID NOT KNOW THAT YOU

32

COULD LOVE THIS MUCH", SHE RECEIVED THE BLESSING. GOD WENT ON FURTHER TO EXPLAIN THAT EVERYTIME THAT THERE IS AN ABORTION, (EVERY 93 SECONDS IN AMERICA), THAT THIS IS NOT ONLY MURDER BUT A BLOOD SACRIFICE TO THE DEVIL (ANTI-CHRIST), AND ADDS TO THE DARKNESS COVERING THE EARTH AND THE PEOPLE. THIS IS ISAIAH 60, DARKNESS WILL COVER THE EARTH AND GROSS DARKNESS THE PEOPLE, THIS DARKNESS IS THE SPIRIT OF DEATH. WOMAN'S CHOICE IS NOTHING BUT A LIE, SPIRIT OF DEATH, FROM THE DEVIL THAT PEOPLE ARE AGREEING WITH, IT IS SIN, AGREEMENT WITH THE SPIRIT OF DEATH. I HAD A YOUNG LADY JUST THE OTHER DAY, TELL ME THAT THIS IS THE REASON SHE LEFT HER CHURCH. THINK ABOUT THIS, EVERYONE IN THAT CHURCH INCLUDING THE PASTOR, ELDERS, DEACONS, AND MEMBERS THAT AGREE WITH THE DEVIL, ARE IN SIN, AND HAVE THE DEVIL'S DNA, SPIRIT OF DEATH. YOU ACTUALLY HAVE A MAN IN THE PULPIT PROMOTING SIN, AGREEMENT WITH THE SPIRIT OF DEATH, WITH THE DEVIL'S DNA. LOOK AT ALL THE PEOPLE IN THE WORLD WHO ARE PROMOTING DEATH BY ABORTION (WOMAN'S CHOICE), THEY ARE IN SIN, AGREEMENT WITH THE DEVIL, THEY ALL HAVE THE DNA, SPIRIT OF DEATH, OF THE DEVIL AND DESPERATELY NEED TO BE SET FREE FROM IT. I MINISTER TO A LOT OF WOMEN AND YOUNG LADIES THAT ARE CONSUMED WITH GUILT AND SHAME AFTER THEIR ABORTIONS, AND THIS CARRIES WITH THEM FOR THE REST OF THEIR LIFE. A LOT OF THESE WOMEN WERE MOLESTED AND RAPED BY FAMILY MEMBERS AND WERE THREATENED TO NEVER TELL ANYONE. THAT THEY WERE DAMAGED GOODS, AND NOBODY WOULD EVER LOVE THEM. AND IN MANY CASES THE WOMEN BELIEVED THEM AND FELL INTO A LIFE OF PROMISCUITY. LISTEN TO ME CLOSELY, GOD WILL NEVER CONDEMN YOU OR ACCUSE YOU, GOD DID NOT CREATE GUILT AND SHAME, THESE ARE LIES, SPIRIT OF DEATH OF THE DEVIL. THE DEVIL WILL USE THESE LIES TO DRAG YOU DEEPER INTO THE DARKNESS, AND INTO DEATH. THE DEVIL WILL

USE WITCHCRAFT TO CONTROL AND DESTROY YOU. JESUS CHRIST LOVES YOU, AND HE WILL ALWAYS LOVE YOU, HE WILL BREAK OFF ALL THESE LIES, OPPRESSION, SPIRIT OF DEATH, OF THE DEVIL AND SET YOU FREE FROM THIS TORMENT, YOU ARE PRECIOUS IN HIS EYES. NOW THAT THIS HAS BEEN REVEALED TO YOU, TAKE A CLOSE LOOK AT THE LEADERS IN WASHINGTON, DC, CAN YOU NOW SEE AND HEAR THE LIES OF THE DEVIL, THE SPIRIT OF DEATH, SPEWING OUT OF THEIR MOUTHS, PROMOTING SIN, PROMOTING DEATH. SINCE ROE VS WADE WAS INSTITUTED OVER 60,000,000 (SIXTY MILLON) BABIES HAVE BEEN SACRIFICED TO THE SPIRIT OF DEATH. THIS MEANS THAT APPROXIMATELY 60,000,000 POTENTIAL WOULD BE MOTHERS AND FATHERS ARE DEALING WITH GUILT AND SHAME (LIES OF THE DEVIL). THIS EQUATES TO APPROXIMATELY 1/3 OF ALL FEMALES IN THE USA HAVE SACRIFICED THEIR BABIES TO THE SPIRIT OF DEATH. NOW, REALIZE THAT THESE FEMALES ARE OUR PRECIOUS DAUGHTERS AND GRANDDAUGHTERS AND THE MALES ARE OUR PRECIOUS SONS AND GRANDSONS. THEY NEED DESPERATELY TO BE SET FREE. ONLY JESUS CHRIST HAS THE POWER AND AUTHORITY OVER THE SPIRIT OF DEATH, TO SET THEM FREE FROM THEIR TORMENT, AND PUT THEIR LIVES BACK TOGETHER. DOES THIS HELP ANSWER YOUR QUESTION OF WHY AMERICA IS IN THE SHAPE THAT IT IS IN, CHOOSE LIFE NOT DEATH.

REBELLION – 501C3 – TAX EXEMPT SLAVE!

WHERE IS THE CHURCH OF JESUS CHRIST? JESUS CHRIST IS HEAD OF HIS CHURCH. THE FEDERAL GOVERNMENT, THE STATE GOVERNMENT, THE COUNTY GOVERNMENT OR ANY GOVERNMENT WHATSOEVER IS NEVER TO BE IN CHARGE OF JESUS CHRIST'S CHURCH. TO MAKE THIS CLEAR, NO PERSON, GROUP, GOVERNMENT, OR ENTITY OF ANY KIND, THIS INCLUDES THE UNITED NATIONS IS EVER TO HAVE AUTHORITY OF THE

CHURCH OF JESUS CHRIST. THIS AUTHORITY BELONGS TO JESUS CHRIST AND HIM ALONE. TODAY, MOST OF THE CHURCHES ARE UNDER THE THUMB OF THE FEDERAL GOVERNMENT, UNDER THE GUISE OF 501C3, TAX EXEMPT STATUS. THIS TAX EXEMPT STATUS ALLOWS THE FEDERAL GOVERNMENT CONTROL OVER WHAT THEY ARE ALLOWED TO PREACH AND WHAT ACTIONS THEY CAN PURSUE. THIS USURPS GOD'S AUTHORITY OVER HIS CHURCH, THIS IS SIN, SPIRIT OF DEATH, AND MUCH CONTROVERSARY HAS COME FROM THIS. IF AT ANY TIME, THE FEDERAL GOVERNMENT OR ANY GOVERNMENT OR ANY ENTITY OF ANY KIND, ESPECIALLY CHURCHES PASSES LAWS OR ORDINANCES OR DECREES OR STATUTES THAT GO AGAINST GOD'S TRUTH, THIS IS SIN, AGREEMENT WITH THE SPIRIT OF DEATH, AND YOU ARE NOT TO BE A PARTAKER OF IT. ONLY THE TRUTH OF JESUS CHRIST CAN SET YOU FREE AND THIS MUST NEVER BE COMPROMISED. THIS OPPRESSION, SPIRIT OF DEATH, ALL THESE LIES **MUST BE BROKEN**, SO THAT ALL OF MANKIND CAN RECEIVE THE TRUTH OF JESUS CHRIST OF HIS AMAZING LOVE AND GRACE TO SET THEM FREE BEFORE IT IS TOO LATE FOR REDEMPTION, CHOOSE LIFE NOT DEATH.

REBELLION – HOMOSEXUALITY – AGAINST GOD'S NATURE!

THE HOLY SPIRIT WENT ON FURTHER TO TALK ABOUT HOMOSEXUALITY. THIS TOTALLY GOES AGAINST THE NATURE OF GOD, AND HIS NATURAL ORDER THAT HE SET IN PLACE, AND AGAIN THIS IS SIN, AGREEMENT WITH THE DEVIL, SPIRIT OF DEATH. THIS IS DEATH, AND NO LIFE CAN COME FROM THIS PRACTICE. ROMANS 1. I MINISTER TO MANY HOMOSEXUALS, AND THEY ARE CONSUMED WITH NOT ONLY GUILT AND SHAME, BUT SUICIDE, SPIRIT OF DEATH. LISTEN CLOSELY TO WHAT I AM SAYING TO YOU, THE DEVIL IS A LIAR. HOMOSEXUALITY AND SUICIDE ARE DEMONIC SPIRITS, SPIRITS OF DEATH, LIES FROM THE

PIT OF HELL. JESUS CHRIST LOVES YOU, AND WILL ALWAYS LOVE YOU AND HE WILL DESTROY ALL OF THIS OPPRESSION, SPIRIT OF DEATH, OFF OF YOU AND SET YOU FREE. EVERYTHING TO DO WITH JESUS CHRIST LEADS TO LIFE, ETERNAL LIFE, AND EVERYTHING TO DO WITH THE DEVIL LEADS TO DEATH, ETERNAL DEATH. LET JESUS CHRIST FORGIVE YOU AND MAKE YOU WHOLE. AGAIN, MANY PEOPLE HAVE LEFT THEIR CHURCH BECAUSE OF THIS PRACTICE BEING CONDONED IN THEIR CHURCH. THE HOLY SPIRIT GAVE ME THIS COUNCIL FOR THEM. TELL THE PEOPLE OF THE CHURCH THAT YOU LOVE THEM, BUT THAT YOU CANNOT AND WILL NOT BE INVOLVED IN THIS SIN. THAT YOU CANNOT SIT UNDER A PREACHER WHO IS PROFESSING SIN, AGREEMENT WITH THE SPIRIT OF DEATH, FROM THE PULPIT. AGAIN, YOU HAVE A PREACHER, ELDERS, DEACONS, AND CHURCH MEMBERS WITH THE DEVIL'S DNA. AND AGAIN, LOOK AT WASHINGTON, DC SPEWING FORTH SAME SEX MARRIAGE, PROMOTING SIN, AGREEMENT WITH THE SPIRIT OF DEATH, AND THIS SIN LEADS TO DEATH, ETERNAL DEATH. THE ANTICHRIST IS A HOMOSEXUAL. DAN 11. PRAISE GOD THAT JESUS CHRIST WILL SET THEM FREE FROM THIS TORMENT NOW, AND THE ETERNAL TORMENT TO COME, CHOOSE LIFE NOT DEATH.

REBELLION – HOOKING UP – EMPTINESS!

SINCE WE HAVE DISCUSSED HOMOSEXUALS, LETS TALK ABOUT HETEROSEXUALS. GOD'S DESIGN IS ALL ABOUT INTIMACY, WHERE TWO BECOME ONE IN LOVE, PEACE, AND JOY. GOD CREATED, INSTITUTED, AND ORDAINED SEXUAL INTERCOURSE FOR A MARRIED MAN AND HIS WIFE. THEY HAVE MADE A COMMITMENT TO EACH OTHER, AND FORMED A COVENANT BETWEEN THEM TO BE FAITHFUL TO EACH OTHER FOREVER. THIS NORMALLY RESULTS IN MORE LIFE, CHILDREN BEING CREATED. ANY SEX OUTSIDE OF HIS DESIGN IS SIN, AGREEMENT WITH THE

SPIRIT OF DEATH, AND OPENS THE DOOR FOR THE DEVIL TO CREATE HAVOC AND ALL KINDS OF HEART ACHES. THESE THINGS MOST OF YOU KNOW. NOW, LETS TALK ABOUT WHAT YOU MAY OR MAY NOT KNOW. EVERYTIME, A MAN AND A WOMAN HAVE SEXUAL INTERCOURSE, TWO BECOME ONE AND A SOUL TIE IS CREATED BETWEEN THEM. HIS SOUL AND HER SOUL ARE JOINED TOGETHER. THIS IS GOD'S DESIGN AND IS A BEAUTIFUL THING, INTIMACY OF LOVE AND ACCEPTANCE. NOW, WITH NUMEROUS PARTNERS THIS BECOMES A DISASTER, THE RESULT IS EMPTINESS. LET ME EXPLAIN WHY, NUMEROUS SEXUAL PARTNERS INVOLVES NUMEROUS SOUL TIES, TODAY THIS IS CALLED HOOKING UP. FOR EXAMPLE, A MAN HAS BEEN INVOLVED IN SIX SEXUAL ENCOUNTERS AND THE WOMAN HAS HAD SIX SEXUAL PARTNERS. THIS RESULTS IN TWELVE SOUL TIES, TOTAL CONFUSION, ALL INTIMACY IS LOST, NO LOVE, NO PEACE, AND NO JOY. NOW BOTH SEXES FIND IT ALMOST IMPOSSIBLE TO FIND THE TRUE LOVE THAT THEY ARE LONGING FOR. SO WHAT DO THEY DO TO FILL THIS EMPTINESS, THEY HAVE MORE SEX AND THIS RESULTS IN MORE AND MORE EMPTINESS. TODAY, MANY ARE LIVING TOGETHER, THIS JUST SEEMS TO BE THE NORMAL THING TO DO. THIS IS OH SO DANGEROUS, THESE RELATIONSHIPS ARE LIVING IN SIN, AGREEMENT WITH THE DEVIL, OR SIMPLY PUT IN AGREEMENT WITH THE SPIRIT OF DEATH, A COVENANT OF DEATH. IN MANY CASES THIS RESULTS IN UNWANTED PREGNANCIES, AND SOMETIMES ABORTIONS, WHICH WE HAVE ALREADY DISCUSSED. NO AMOUNT OF SEX, ALCOHOL AND DRUGS WILL FILL THE VOID OF EMPTINESS. HALLELUJAH, THERE IS AN ANSWER, ALL THAT EMPTINESS CAN BE FILLED WITH THE LOVE AND AMAZING GRACE OF JESUS CHRIST. ALL YOU NEED TO DO IS CONFESS, REPENT OF YOUR SIN, AGREEMENT WITH THE SPIRIT OF DEATH, AND LIVE ACCORDING TO GOD'S WORD AND RECEIVE HIS INTIMACY, LOVE, PEACE AND JOY. LET JESUS CHRIST

37

LOVE ON YOU AND YOUR EMPTINESS WILL DISAPPEAR, AND YOUR LIFE WILL FLOURISH, CHOOSE LIFE NOT DEATH.

REBELLION – NATURAL ORDER – MAN AND WOMAN!

THE HOLY SPIRIT WENT ON FURTHER TO TALK ABOUT GOD'S NATURAL ORDER FOR MANKIND. A MAN NEEDS A WOMAN, AND A WOMAN NEEDS A MAN, THIS IS GOD'S PLAN TO FULFILL EACH OTHER AND POPULATE THE EARTH. MAN IS TO BE THE HEAD OF THE HOUSE HOLD, THE SPIRITUAL LEADER OF THE FAMILY. MAN IS TO LOVE AND CHERISH HIS WIFE AND FAMILY AS JESUS CHRIST LOVES AND TAKES CARE OF HIS FAMILY, HIS CHURCH. THE MAN IS TO BE THE COVERING OVER HIS WIFE AND CHILDREN, HE IS THEIR PROTECTOR. HE IS TO PROTECT THEM SPIRITUALLY FROM THE DEMONIC AND NATURALLY FROM THE EVIL MANIFESTING IN MANKIND. WHEN THIS NATURAL ORDER IS USURPED AND TURNED UPSIDE DOWN, THE SIN, AGREEMENT WITH THE SPIRIT OF DEATH, OF REBELLION RAISES ITS UGLY HEAD AND THE DEVIL GETS IN. THIS IS ONE OF THE MAIN REASONS FOR THE HIGH DIVORCE RATES AND THE CHILDREN PAY THE PRICE FOR THEIR PARENTS REBELLION. NOW THAT REBELLION HAS ENTERED IN, THE CHILDREN PICK UP ON IT, AND IF IT IS NOT STOPPED THIS REBELLION, SPIRIT OF DEATH, IS CARRIED FORWARD TO FUTURE GENERATIONS. THIS RESULTS IN ADDICTIONS OF ALL KINDS, HIGH DIVORCE RATES, HOMOSEXUALITY, AND PERVERSIONS OF ALL KINDS AGAINST THE NATURAL ORDER THAT GOD PUT INTO PLACE, CHOOSE LIFE NOT DEATH.

REBELLION – EPIDEMIC OF DEATH

MANKIND IS PREOCCUPIED, CONSUMED, AND FASCINATED WITH DEATH, THE DEMONIC SPIRIT OF SUICIDE. WE ARE EXPERIENCING NOW AN EPIDEMIC ACROSS THIS NATION WITH YOUNG FEMALES, AS YOUNG AS ELEMENTARY SCHOOL. THIS EPIDEMIC IS

38

EXPLOSIVE IN HIGH SCHOOL AND COLLEGE. THIS EPIDEMIC INVOLVES PRESCRIPTION DRUGS FOR ANXIETY AND DEPRESSION. SO MANY YOUNG FEMALES ARE CAUGHT UP IN THE WORLDLY VISION, SPIRIT OF DEATH, VERSUS GODLY VISION, SPIRIT OF LIFE, AND THEY CANNOT HANDLE REALITY. OUR YOUNG MEN ARE TURNING TO ALCOHOL AND DRUGS TO HANDLE REALITY. OUR YOUTH ARE BEING BOMBARDED AND THEY ARE CONFUSED, DISORIENTED, AND THEY ARE SEARCHING FOR A SENSE OF PEACE AND STABILITY IN THEIR LIVES. HERE IS ONE SIMPLE EXPLANATION.... OUR YOUTH, BOMBARDED DAILY WITH SIN (AGREEMENT WITH THE SPIRIT OF DEATH), MANY KNOWING BETTER ARE CHOOSING TO GO WITH THE WORLD, AGREEING WITH THE LIES THAT THEY ARE SEEING AND HEARING, AND THE ONLY WAY THAT THEY THINK THEY CAN DEAL WITH THEIR REALITY IS TO TRY AND CHANGE THEIR REALITY WITH DRUGS AND ALCOHOL. OUR GODLESS CULTURE, IN AGREEMENT WITH DEATH, THE DEVIL, IS BEING TAUGHT IN OUR SCHOOLS, AND PROFESSED BY THE MEDIA, AND THE RESULT IS THAT OUR YOUTH ARE BEING SEPARATED FROM THEIR CREATOR. THEY ARE BEING SEPARATED FROM THE SOURCE OF LIFE, LOVE, PEACE AND JOY. OUR GODLESS CULTURE IS CONSUMED WITH SELF AND DEATH. OUR YOUTH ARE BEING INDOCTRINATED WITH DEATH, AND THIS IS DESTROYING OUR YOUTH. EVERYTHING ABOUT THE DEVIL DEALS WITH DEATH. EVERYTHING ABOUT JESUS CHRIST IS LIFE, LIFE MORE ABUNDANTLY, ETERNAL LIFE. IF ALL OUR YOUTH HEAR ABOUT IS DEATH, DEATH, AND MORE DEATH, NO WONDER THEY ARE DEPRESSED AND LOOKING FOR A WAY OUT. **ONLY THE LOVE OF JESUS CHRIST BY THE POWER OF THE HOLY SPIRIT CAN BREAK OFF ALL THE OPPRESSION, SPIRIT OF DEATH, OF THE DEVIL, AND SET OUR YOUTH FREE!**

I WAS IN A MEETING WITH GENERAL JERRY BOYKIN AND TODAY'S LEADERS OF THE CHURCH. I WAS ASKED.... WHY DID

83% OF THEIR YOUTH THAT GO TO COLLEGE FALL FROM THE FAITH. I EXPLAINED THAT THEIR YOUTH HAD NEVER BEEN LED THE HOLY SPIRIT TO BEGIN WITH. THEY HAD HEARD ABOUT HIM, BUT NEVER HAD THE SUPERNATURAL EXPERIENCE, NEVER FELT THE LOVE, PEACE, AND JOY OF HIS PRESENCE. THEY HAD NEVER EXPERIENCED HIS POWER TO SET THEM FREE, AND KEEP THEM FREE, AND USE THEM TO HELP OTHERS GET SET FREE.

OUR YOUTH ARE BRAINWASHED WITH LIES OF DEATH AND THIS IS TOTALLY AGAINST THE NATURE OF GOD. OUR ADULTS ARE ALSO CAUGHT UP IN THE DEATH THEME. I AM AMAZED HOW MANY ADULTS ARE ON PRESCRIPTION DRUGS FOR ANXIETY AND DEPRESSION, THIS LEADS TO ALCOHOL, AND DRUG ABUSE. IT IS STAGGERING HOW MANY THAT I MINISTER TO THAT HAVE LOST THEIR WAY IN LIFE AND HAVE BECOME BITTER. LIFE IS NOT WHAT THEY THOUGHT IT WOULD BE AND THEY HAVE LOST THEIR WAY. IT IS VERY CLEAR, WHEN YOU ARE SEPARATED FROM THE SOURCE OF ALL LIFE, LOVE, PEACE, AND JOY, YOU BECOME BITTER AGAINST LIFE. THIS SHOWS UP IN THEIR RELATIONSHIPS WITH THEIR SPOUSES, CHILDREN, FRIENDS, WORK ENVIRONMENT, AND EVERYONE THEY COME IN CONTACT WITH. THIS DEATH SPIRAL IS CONTAGIOUS UNTIL IT IS BROKEN AND THEY ARE SET FREE BY JESUS CHRIST.

NOW, ALL OF YOU CAN SEE WHAT WE HAVE DONE BY REMOVING JESUS CHRIST FROM OUR SCHOOL SYSTEM, WORK PLACE, FAMILY AND EVERYDAY LIVES. WE WATCH AND CONDONE THE DEATH LIES OF HOLLYWOOD AND THE MEDIA AND ELECT POLITICIANS THAT SPEW FORTH THE LIES OF THE DEVIL, DEATH BEING THEIR PRIMARY CONCERN. AND WITH ALL OF THIS WE WONDER WHY OUR CHILDREN ARE SO LOST AND SEARCHING. **WAKE UP!**.... TURN AWAY FROM DEATH, CONFESS, REPENT, AND JESUS CHRIST WILL SET YOU AND YOUR CHILDREN FREE, JESUS

CHRIST, THE ANSWER, ETERNAL LIFE. I PERSONALLY HAVE BEEN BLESSED TO SEE MANY SET FREE FROM DEATH TO LIFE. YOU TOO, CAN PICK UP THE CROSS, BE SET FREE AND HELP OTHERS BE SET FREE TO LIFE, ETERNAL LIFE. THERE IS NO GREATER FEELING AND PURPOSE ON THIS EARTH THAN TO SEE THE LOST SAVED, SET FREE SPIRITUALLY, SOULFULLY, AND PHYSICALLY, SET FREE TO LIFE, LOVE, PEACE, JOY, AND ETERNAL LIFE.

NOW LISTEN CLOSELY TO A REVELATION FROM THE HOLY SPIRIT CONCERNING OUR MILITARY, VETS, AND ACTIVE DUTY. THE HOLY SPIRIT REVEALED WHY THE SPIRIT OF SUICIDE IS RUNNING RAMPANT IN THE MILITARY. OUR MILITARY IS FOCUSED ON DEATH, WHICH IS CONTRARY TO GOD AND LIFE. THEY HAVE BEEN INVOLVED IN DEATH ON BOTH SIDES, KILLING THE ENEMY AND WATCHING THEIR OWN FRIENDS DIE. THIS DEATH HAS SO TRAUMATIZED THEM, THAT DEATH HAS BECOME NORMAL, AND THE SPIRIT OF SUICIDE TO THEM IS THE NORMAL THING TO DO. THIS REQUIRES INTENSE SPIRITUAL WARFARE TO BREAK IT AND AT A MINIMUM DAILY CONFESSION, REPENTENCE, AND COMMUNION TO BE FREE AND STAY SET FREE. JESUS CHRIST CAN AND WILL DO IT FOR THEM. THE HOLY SPIRIT ALSO REVEALED TO ME THAT OUR YOUTH ARE BEING CAUGHT UP IN THE SPIRIT OF DEATH. **EVERYDAY, TEENAGERS ARE COMMITTING SUICIDE**. THIS IS BECOMING MORE NORMAL TO THEM. THIS COVENANT OF DEATH MUST BE BROKEN.

NOW, PLEASE DON'T MISUNDERSTAND, I AM NOT ACCUSING ANYONE OF ANYTHING, I AM LAYING OUT THE FACTS IN LOVE. IT IS THIS SIMPLE, IF GOD (LIFE) GOES OUT, THEN THE DEVIL (DEATH) MOVES IN. THIS IS THE FACT THAT WE MUST DEAL WITH. UNDERSTAND, ALL OF CREATION LIES IN THE BALANCE, CHOOSE LIFE NOT DEATH, WE MUST END THIS COVENANT WITH DEATH.

GOD'S NATURAL ORDER IS NOT TO HINDER YOU, BUT TO LEAD YOU TO JESUS CHRIST, LIFE, LOVE, PEACE AND JOY. WHAT WE HAVE JUST DISCUSSED ARE ALL LIES OF THE DEVIL THAT GO AGAINST THE NATURAL ORDER OF GOD, THAT HAVE ENTRAPPED AND MADE SLAVES OF THE PEOPLE OF THIS WORLD. THESE LIES HAVE DESTROYED NOT ONLY THE CHILDREN BUT THE ADULTS. REALIZE, GOD WILL NEVER USE GUILT AND SHAME AGAINST YOU, THIS IS STRAIGHT FROM HELL. JESUS CHRIST WILL FORGIVE YOU, SET YOU FREE AND GIVE YOU YOUR LIFE BACK.

PERSONAL CHALLENGE....

DO YOU LOVE THEM ENOUGH AND HAVE THE COURAGE TO GIVE THEM THE TRUTH? THERE IS ONLY ONE ANSWER.... JESUS CHRIST, THE ANSWER, ETERNAL LIFE, HIS AMAZING LOVE AND ACCEPTANCE, HIS AMAZING GRACE TO SET YOU FREE TO ETERNAL LIFE. THIS IS YOUR CHOICE TO MAKE, LIFE, FREEDOM, LOVE, PEACE, AND JOY ARE ALL IN THE INTIMACY OF BECOMING ONE WITH JESUS CHRIST, CHOOSE LIFE NOT DEATH.

I PROMISE YOU AS A PASTOR OF THE GOSPEL OF JESUS CHRIST, IN THE INTIMACY OF BECOMING ONE WITH JESUS CHRIST, YOU WILL FIND YOUR PURPOSE AND YOUR REASON FOR LIVING ON THIS EARTH. SUDDENLY, IT WILL BE AS IF A LIGHT BULB GOES OFF AND YOU WILL KNOW AND SAY, OH MY.... JESUS CHRIST LOVES ME, HE HEARS ME, HE PAYS ATTENTION TO ME, HE HAS TIME FOR ME, JESUS CHRIST REALLY DOES LOVE ME...AND YOU WILL NEVER BE THE SAME.

THIS WAS MY PERSONAL EXPERIENCE THAT CHANGED ME FOREVER. I WILL NEVER FORGET THAT MOMENT.

42

YAHWEH 'S LOVE & ACCEPTANCE!

YAHWEH LOVES AND ACCEPTS YOU, JUST AS YOU ARE, YOU ARE NOT ALONE. YAHWEH WILL NEVER ACCUSE OR CONDEMN YOU. JESUS CHRIST WILL ALWAYS ACCEPT YOU REGARDLESS OF WHAT YOU HAVE DONE. JESUS CHRIST PREACHED, CONFESS AND REPENT, AND HE WILL FORGIVE YOUR SIN (AGREEMENT WITH THE DEVIL, SPIRIT OF DEATH) WASH IT ALL AWAY AS IF IT NEVER HAPPENED, AND FILL THE VOID IN YOUR SOUL WITH HIMSELF, SPIRIT OF LIFE, ETERNAL LIFE, LOVE, PEACE, AND JOY. YOU ARE PRICELESS TO HIM, YOU ARE MADE IN HIS IMAGE, THE IMAGE OF THE GREAT I AM. JN 3 THIS IS VERY IMPORTANT FOR YOU TO UNDERSTAND. THE DEVIL IS A LIAR, DO NOT LET HIM DECEIVE YOU INTO FEARING YAHWEH. FEAR IS NOT REAL, IT IS A LIE, SPIRIT OF DEATH, OF THE DEVIL. REMEMBER, WITH THE DEVIL, "NOTHING IS AT IT SEEMS", ONLY THE LIGHT OF THE TRUTH OF JESUS CHRIST AND HIS ETERNAL LIFE COVENANT, CAN SET YOU FREE TO ETERNAL LIFE ON EARTH AS IT IS IN HEAVEN. **THE DEVIL PLAYS MIND GAMES, AND YAHWEH MOVES IN HEART CHANGE.** FATHER YAHWEH WANTS ONLY THE BEST FOR YOU, HE SENT HIS SON JESUS CHRIST, SO YOU COULD HAVE ETERNAL LIFE. JN 3 **JESUS CHRIST IS NOT A MAN-MADE ORDAINED RELIGION. JESUS CHRIST IS THE LIVING SON OF YAHWEH. JESUS CHRIST IS YAHWEH. JESUS CHRIST IS THE LIVING WORD OF YAHWEH.** THE WORD OF YAHWEH, THE HOLY BIBLE, IS ALIVE. JESUS CHRIST CAME TO DESTROY THE LIES AND OPPRESSION, SPIRIT OF DEATH OF THE DEVIL, REVEAL, MAKE KNOWN, SHOW US THE WAY, AND LEAD US TO FATHER YAHWEH, ETERNAL LIFE. "I AM THE WAY, THE TRUTH, AND THE LIFE, AND NO MAN COMETH UNTO THE FATHER BUT BY ME."JN 14 **JESUS CHRIST WANTS FAR MORE THAN A RELATIONSHIP WITH YOU, HE WANTS INTIMACY (LIFE, LOVE AND ACCEPTANCE), WHERE TWO BECOME ONE TOGETHER. JN 17**

43

"INTIMACY BREATHES EXPECTATION" THS (THE HOLY SPIRIT)

"WHATEVER YOU FOCUS ON, YOU BECOME. WHATEVER YOU FOCUS ON, YOU AUTOMATICALLY RECEIVE." THS
YAHWEH LOVES EVERYONE THE SAME, AND HE SEES THEIR HEARTS AS THEY REALLY ARE. HE SEES THROUGH THE DARKNESS AND HAZE (LIES, SPIRIT OF DEATH OF THE DEVIL). **JESUS CHRIST SEES YOU IN ONE OF TWO WAYS, A SOUL THAT HAS FOUND HIS WAY TO ETERNAL LIFE, AND A SOUL THAT HAS LOST HIS WAY TO ETERNAL LIFE. NOT A LOST SOUL, BUT A SOUL THAT IS TRAPPED WITH THE SPIRIT OF DEATH, THAT HAS LOST HIS WAY. THIS SOUL CAN BE REDEEMED BACK TO JESUS CHRIST ANYTIME UNTIL HIS LAST BREATH OF LIFE ON THIS EARTH. 6/17 THS**

YOUR SOUL IS YOUR MIND, YOUR WILL, AND YOUR EMOTIONS. YOUR SPIRIT IS YAHWEH'S SPIRIT IN YOU. THE HOLY SPIRIT IS YAHWEH, THE BREATH OF YAHWEH, GIVER OF LIFE, THE SPIRIT OF JESUS CHRIST, THE SPIRIT OF ETERNAL LIFE. **YOUR FAITH IS BELIEVING AND RECEIVING, TRUSTING, OBEYING, AND ACTING ON YAHWEH'S HOLY LIVING WORD OF TRUTH, AGREEMENT WITH JESUS CHRIST.** YOUR SIN IS WHEN YOU ARE IN AGREEMENT WITH THE SPIRIT OF DEATH. YOU ARE EITHER IN AGREEMENT WITH JESUS CHRIST OR THE DEVIL, THERE IS NO IN BETWEEN. JN 15 YOU EITHER HAVE JESUS CHRIST'S DNA, SPIRIT OF LIFE OR THE DEVILS, SPIRIT OF DEATH THERE IS NO IN BETWEEN. THINK LONG AND HARD ABOUT THIS REVOLUTIONARY TRUTH, WHO'S DNA DO YOU CARRY?
NOW, ASK THE HOLY SPIRIT, THE SPIRIT OF JESUS CHRIST TO REVEAL THE TRUTH OF JESUS CHRIST TO YOU. 1COR. 12
JESUS CHRIST SAID "LOVE ONE ANOTHER AS I HAVE LOVED YOU." JN 15 "LOVE NEVER FAILS" 1COR 13

THE KEY: LEARN TO LOVE, LEARN TO ACCEPT LOVE, AND LEARN TO LOVE AND ACCEPT EACH OTHER INTO THE KINGDOM OF YAHWEH. ! JN 15 CHOOSE LIFE NOT DEATH!

ETERNAL LIFE IS THE LIVING WORD, THE GOSPEL OF THE KINGDOM OF YAHWEH. ETERNAL LIFE IS INTIMACY (LOVE AND ACCEPTANCE) BETWEEN YOU AND YAHWEH. ETERNAL LIFE IS YAHWEH'S NATURE, HIS WILL FOR YOU, YOUR FREEDOM, YOUR GIFT, YOUR BLESSING, YOUR REWARD, YOUR DESTINY, AND HIS GLORY IN YOU ON THIS EARTH AS IT IS IN HEAVEN. 1JN3

STEP BY STEP I AM GOING TO TEACH YOU HOW TO BECOME A TRUE SON OF YAHWEH, THE DEEP TRUTHS OF YAHWEH. HOW MUCH YAHWEH LOVES AND ACCEPTS YOU, HOW TO BE SET FREE, RECEIVE ETERNAL LIFE AND HOW TO BECOME ONE WITH JESUS CHRIST. HOW TO BECOME HIS WITNESS IN ALL THE EARTH, PREACHING THE LIVING GOSPEL, MOVING IN HIS LIVING WORD, AND POWER OF THE HOLY SPIRIT, SPEAKING IN THE LANGUAGE OF ETERNAL LIFE, LIFTING PEOPLE UP INTO HIS PRESENCE, AND OPERATING IN HIS MIRACLES OF RESTORATION, SPIRIT, SOUL, AND BODY. I AM GOING TO TEACH YOU HOW TO DESTROY ALL OF THE OPPRESSION, SPIRIT OF DEATH, OF THE DEVIL WITH YAHWEH'S TRUTH. **JESUS CHRIST HAS ALL POWER AND ALL AUTHORITY, THE DEVIL HAS NONE.**

YAHWEH IS LOVE!

YAHWEH IS LOVE. 1JN4. YAHWEH IS YOUR HEAVENLY FATHER, AND YOU ARE HIS MOST PRECIOUS CREATION. OUT OF ALL THAT YAHWEH CREATED, WHICH IS EVERYTHING, YOU ARE MADE IN HIS OWN IMAGE. GEN.2 **FATHER YAHWEH LOVES YOU AS MUCH AS HE LOVES JESUS CHRIST. JN17.** JESUS CHRIST SAID IF YOU LOVE ME, AND OBEY ME, THE FATHER AND I WILL MOVE IN WITH YOU,

MAKING YOU OUR HOME, AND WE WILL BECOME ONE TOGETHER. JN17 EYES HAVE NOT SEEN, EARS HAVE NOT HEARD, AND OUR MINDS CANNOT CONCEIVE WHAT YAHWEH HAS PREPARED FOR THOSE WHO LOVE HIM. 1COR2 YAHWEH WANTS TO SPEND ETERNAL LIFE WITH YOU NOW ON EARTH AS WELL AS IN HEAVEN, THIS IS YOUR CHOICE. MAT6
EMBRACING YAHWEH'S REVOLUTIONARY TRUTH WILL HELP YOU UNDERSTAND, KNOW AS YOU ARE FULLY KNOWN, EXPERIENCE AND BECOME ONE WITH THE AMAZING LOVE AND ACCEPTANCE, ETERNAL LIFE OF FATHER YAHWEH, HIS SON JESUS CHRIST, AND HIS HOLY SPIRIT. **OUT OF THIS INTIMACY COMES GREAT EXPECTATION.**

YAHWEH'S TRUTH!

THE BIBLE, YAHWEH'S HOLY LIVING WORD OF TRUTH, MAKES IT VERY CLEAR, IN THE BEGINNING YAHWEH CREATED THE HEAVENS AND THE EARTH. GEN 1 "IF IT IS NOT IN HEAVEN, THEN YAHWEH DID NOT CREATE IT ON EARTH."1/18THS YAHWEH CREATED EVERYTHING AND NOTHING WAS CREATED THAT HE DID NOT CREATE, AND EVERYTHING HE CREATES IS GOOD. JN1 THERE IS ONLY ONE YAHWEH, FATHER YAHWEH, HIS SON JESUS CHRIST (CHRIST MEANS THE ANOINTED ONE), AND HIS HOLY SPIRIT (THE BREATH OF GOD). 1JN5 JESUS CHRIST AND THE HOLY SPIRIT CAME FORTH OUT OF THE BOSOM OF THE FATHER. JN1 THESE THREE ARE THE ONE TRUE CREATOR OF ALL CREATION AND ALL THREE AGREE AND ARE ONE IN ETERNAL LIFE. 1JN5 ALL OTHER SO CALLED GODS ARE FALSE MINIONS OF THE DEVIL. 1JN3 DO NOT BE DECEIVED, WHATEVER GOD YOU WORSHIP, THAT SPIRIT WILL COME FORTH OUT OF YOU. JESUS CHRIST IS LIFE, LOVE, PEACE, AND JOY, (ETERNAL LIFE). THE DEVIL IS DEATH, STEAL, KILL AND DESTROY, (ETERNAL DAMNATION). JN10 FATHER YAHWEH

46

SO LOVES AND ACCEPTS YOU, THAT HE SENT HIS ONLY BEGOTTEN SON JESUS CHRIST TO SET YOU FREE. JN3 JESUS CHRIST SO LOVES AND ACCEPTS YOU, HE CAME TO EARTH FROM HEAVEN, AND TOOK THE FORM OF FLESH TO SET YOU FREE FROM ALL THE LIES AND OPPRESSION, SPIRIT OF DEATH OF THE DEVIL. 1JN1 HE WAS BORN OF HIS EARTHLY JEWISH MOTHER, THE VIRGIN MARY, AND HIS HEAVENLY FATHER, THROUGH THE POWER OF THE HOLY SPIRIT. LK1 HE DIED ON THE CROSS, FOR THE TOTAL REMISSION OF YOUR SIN (AGREEMENT WITH THE DEVIL, SPIRIT OF DEATH). HIS PRECIOUS BLOOD WAS SHED, FORGIVES YOUR SIN, WASHES YOU CLEAN, SETS YOU FREE, RESTORES YOU ALL IN ALL, SPIRIT, SOUL, AND BODY. 1JN1 HE AROSE FROM THE GRAVE THROUGH THE POWER OF THE HOLY SPIRIT. THIS IS HOLY SPIRIT'S VICTORY OVER DEATH.   VICTORY OVER DEATH IS ETERNAL LIFE. 1JN1 JESUS CHRIST ASCENDED BACK TO HIS FATHER YAHWEH IN HEAVEN AND SITS AT HIS RIGHT HAND. HE ENDURED ALL OF THIS TORMENT FOR ONE PURPOSE, TO MAKE IT POSSIBLE FOR YAHWEH, THE HOLY SPIRIT, TO COME AND LIVE INSIDE YOU, BLESS YOU BY MAKING YOU HIS HOME, AND WITH YOUR PERMISSION A COMMAND BASE OF OPERATIONS TO TRAIN YOU TO BECOME A TRUE SON OR DAUGHTER OF YAHWEH ENDUED WITH HIS POWER TO SPEAK AND ACT ON LIVING SPIRIT WORDS OF TRUTH AND LOVE TO DESTROY THE WORKS, SPIRIT OF DEATH OF THE DEVIL, MIRACLES OF RESTORATION ABOUND, AND TO SET ALL MANKIND FREE TO ETERNAL LIFE. REMEMBER, JESUS CHRIST IS COMING BACK TO TAKE HIS FAMILY HOME TO HEAVEN, ETERNAL LIFE. JESUS CHRIST IS ALSO COMING BACK TO THIS EARTH, AT THE END OF THE AGE, WITH HIS SAINTS, TO RULE AND REIGN FOR A 1000 YEARS. JESUS CHRIST PAID THE PRICE FOR YOUR SIN WITH HIS OWN BLOOD. YOU ARE SET FREE (SAVED) BY HIS WORKS AND AMAZING GRACE. YOUR WORKS WILL NOT SAVE YOU, BUT THEY ARE THE FRUIT OF YOU BEING SAVED. EPH 5 YOU TRULY BECOME ONE WITH JESUS CHRIST IN ETERNAL LIFE WHEN YOU CONFESS AND REPENT OF YOUR SIN, SPIRIT OF DEATH,

RECEIVE JESUS CHRIST, ENLIST IN HIS ARMY, SPEAK FORTH HIS LIVING WORDS OF TRUTH AND YOU DO HIS MIRACLES AND SET HIS PEOPLE FREE. JAM1 THE POWER OF THE LIVING WORD IS IN THE SPOKEN WORD. MK11 "FOR THE WAGES OF SIN IS DEATH, BUT THE GIFT OF YAHWEH IS ETERNAL LIFE THROUGH JESUS CHRIST OUR LORD."R6

YAHWEH'S MARCHING ORDERS!

YAHWEH'S MARCHING ORDERS, SHARE MY LOVE (ETERNAL LIFE), LIFT THEM UP INTO MY PRESENCE AND GET OUT OF THE WAY, SET MY PEOPLE FREE, SET MY PEOPLE FREE, SET MY PEOPLE FREE. YOU ARE NOW BEING LIFTED UP INTO HIS PRESENCE, THE PRESENCE OF THE CREATOR. JESUS CHRIST NEVER STOPS CREATING, SO IN HIS PRESENCE YOU AUTOMATICALLY GET RECREATED OR RESTORED. **THE HOLY SPIRIT IS NOT JUST IN YOUR HEART, HE IS IN EVERY CELL IN YOUR BODY, FROM THE TOP OF YOUR HEAD TO THE SOLES OF YOUR FEET.** EVERY CELL IN YOUR BODY IS ACTIVATED AND RESTORED WHEN YOU SPEAK FORTH HIS LIVING WORDS, THEY BECOME ALIVE IN ALL THE CELLS IN YOUR BODY, RESTORATION OF ALL IN ALL, AND MIRACLES ABOUND, FREEDOM FOR YOUR SPIRIT, SOUL, AND BODY.

MIRACLES REVEALED: OPERATION OF THE HOLY SPIRIT IN EVERY CELL IN YOUR BODY!

VIP! LISTEN CLOSELY TO HOW THIS TAKES PLACE. THIS IS EXTREMELY IMPORTANT AND REVEALED BY THE HOLY SPIRIT. WHEN YOU WERE CONCEIVED, THE HOLY SPIRIT BREATHED LIFE INTO YOU, THE SAME HOLY SPIRIT BREATHES LIFE WHEREVER HE GOES. WHEN YOU SPEAK FORTH SPIRIT WORDS OF LIFE, THE

ATMOSPHERE BECOMES SATURATED WITH THE HOLY SPIRIT. YOU BREATHE IN THE HOLY SPIRIT, THE SAME WAY THAT YOU BREATHE IN OXYGEN. YOU BREATHE THE HOLY SPIRIT INTO YOUR LUNGS. THE HOLY SPIRIT IS PICKED UP IN THE BLOOD AND IS CARRIED THROUGHOUT THE BODY INTO EVERY CELL. THE MORE INTENSE THE SATURATION OF THE HOLY SPIRIT, THE QUICKER THE BODY RESTORES BREATHING IN LIFE, ETERNAL LIFE. WHEN A TRUE SON OF YAHWEH, LAYS HANDS ON YOU AND TRANSFERS YAHWEH'S ANOINTING, SPEAKING FORTH LIVING SPIRIT WORDS OF LIFE, THESE WORDS ARE BREATHED IN, RESTORATION OF LIFE BEGINS THROUGHOUT THE ENTIRE BODY. THIS IS REGARDLESS OF WHO YOU ARE, CHRISTIAN, MUSLIM, HINDU, BUDHIST, ATHEIST, ETC., YAHWEH LOVES EVERYONE THE SAME. THESE SPIRIT WORDS OF LIFE DESTROY THE LIES OF THE DEVIL. EYES ARE OPENED TO WHAT IS REAL AND WHAT IS TRUE. THEY CAN NOW SEE AND HEAR THE TRUTH OF JESUS CHRIST, BREATHE IN LIFE, AND THEIR SPIRITS, SOULS, AND BODIES ARE REFRESHED AND RESTORED, MIRACLES ABOUND. THIS IS A GREAT MYSTERY OF HIS MIRACLES REVEALED IN THESE END TIMES.

A MIRACLE IS THE LIGHT OF THE TRUTH REVEALED, THE TRUTH DESTROYS THE LIE, SPIRIT OF DEATH, AND THE LIGHT OF THE TRUTH DESTROYS THE DARKNESS. MIRACLES ONLY HAPPEN IN THE PRESENCE OF JESUS CHRIST WHO IS THE LIGHT. NOW YOU BEGIN TO SEE WHAT IS REAL AND WHAT IS NOT REAL, WHAT IS TRUE AND WHAT IS NOT TRUE.

MIRACLE TESTIMONIES!

THESE ARE A FEW PEOPLE WHO HAVE BEEN RESTORED BY THE UNLIMITED LOVE OF FATHER YAHWEH, JESUS CHRIST AND THE HOLY SPIRIT. LISTEN CLOSELY TO THEIR TESTIMONIES, THEIR MIRACLES OF HOW THEY WERE RESTORED SPIRIT, SOUL, AND BODY., THEY WERE SET FREE FROM THE OPPRESSION, SPIRIT OF DEATH OF THE DEVIL.

PASTOR CLINT HARRIS, RESTORED FROM PANCREATIC CANCER, AND THE SECOND TIME RAISED FROM THE DEAD, MIRACLE AFTER MIRACLE THAT THE DOCTORS TOLD HIS WIFE WOULD NEVER HAPPEN. THE MIRACLE HAPPENED AND HE IS BACK IN THE PULPIT PREACHING.

MRS. JOAN ERWIN, WIFE OF MARK ERWIN, US AMBASSADOR RETIRED. JOAN FIRST BROUGHT HER RELATIVE AND HIS EYE SIGHT WAS RESTORED, AND THEN HER BODY WAS RESTORED FROM CANCER, AND SHE IS TRAVELLING AROUND THE WORLD.

MRS. NAJMA CURRIMJEE, WIFE OF BASHIR OF THE REPUBLIC OF MAURITIUS. NAJMA IS THE 45TH DIRECT DESCENDANT OF MOHAMMAD. WHEN SHE CAME THOUSANDS OF MILES, SHE WAS IN SUCH PAIN, AND WITHIN MINUTES ALL HER PAIN WAS GONE AND SHE WAS WALKING AROUND THE ROOM, AND HER BODY WAS RESTORED.

MISS AMI HARIYANI, SHE IS HINDU, AND HER NECKBONES HAD BEEN FUSED TOGETHER SINCE BIRTH, AND SHE HAD DIFFICULTY MOVING HER HEAD FROM SIDE TO SIDE, HER NECK WAS RELEASED AND SHE NOW HAS NATURAL MOVEMENT. ALSO HER KNEE WAS DAMAGED, AND SHE COULD NOT WALK UP AND DOWN THE STAIRS. HER KNEE WAS RESTORED.

MR. PETE MCDANIEL, ADDICTION PROBLEM, SET FREE AND NOW HAS HIS OWN BUSINESS.

MRS. DORIS HEATON, WIFE OF PASTOR JAMES, TWO HEART ATTACKS, AND HER SPIRIT LEFT HER BODY INTO THE HANDS OF JESUS CHRIST AND SHE WILL TELL YOU ABOUT THE LOVE SHE FELT FLOWING THROUGH HER, AND THEN RAISED FROM THE DEAD.

SIGNS, WONDERS, & MIRACLES!

JESUS CHRIST MADE IT CLEAR IN THE GOSPEL OF MARK 16. "AND HE SAID UNTO THEM. GO YE INTO ALL THE WORLD, AND PREACH THE GOSPEL TO EVERY CREATURE. HE THAT BELIEVETH AND IS BAPTIZED SHALL BE SAVED; BUT HE THAT BELIEVETH NOT SHALL BE DAMNED. AND THESE SIGNS WILL FOLLOW THEM THAT BELIEVE; IN MY NAME SHALL THEY CAST OUT DEVILS; AND THEY SHALL SPEAK WITH NEW TONGUES; THEY SHALL TAKE UP SERPENTS AND IF THEY DRINK ANY DEADLY THING, IT SHALL NOT HURT THEM; THEY SHALL LAY HANDS ON THE SICK, AND THEY SHALL RECOVER. SO THEN AFTER JESUS HAD SPOKEN UNTO THEM, HE WAS RECEIVED UP INTO HEAVEN, AND SAT ON THE RIGHT HAND OF YAHWEH. AND THEY WENT FORTH, AND

PREACHED EVERYWHERE, JESUS CHRIST WORKING WITH THEM
AND CONFIRMING THE WORD WITH SIGNS FOLLOWING, AMEN".
SIGNS, WONDERS, AND MIRACLES ARE HAPPENING NOW, THIS IS
THE REVOLUTION OF LIFE, LOVE AND ACCEPTANCE. MARK 16

JESUS CHRIST LIFE, LOVE, PEACE, AND JOY!

JESUS CHRIST LOVES YOU AND HE WILL ACCEPT YOU JUST AS YOU
ARE. JESUS CHRIST WILL HEAL AND RESTORE YOUR BROKENNESS,
PUT YOU BACK TOGETHER AND MAKE YOU HIS MASTERPIECE.
JN14 JESUS CHRIST IS LIFE, FORGIVENESS, LOVE, PEACE, JOY,
MERCY, GRACE, ETERNAL LIFE, THE SUPERNATURAL POWER OF
CREATION ITSELF, UNLIMITED LOVE. THIS IS NOT WHAT HE HAS,
BUT WHO HE IS, THAT IS WHY JESUS CHRIST IS THE ONLY WAY. "I
AM THE WAY, THE TRUTH, AND THE LIFE; NO MAN COMETH TO
THE FATHER BUT BY ME." JN 14 JESUS CHRIST WILL NEVER
SHAME YOU, ACCUSE, OR CONDEMN YOU. HE WILL NEVER PUT
YOU ON A GUILT TRIP. THIS IS WHY REGARDLESS OF WHAT YOU
HAVE DONE, HE WILL ALWAYS LOVE AND ACCEPT YOU, THIS IS
WHO HE IS. SURRENDER YOUR ALL TO JESUS CHRIST AND HE
WILL GIVE YOU ETERNAL LIFE ON EARTH AS IT IS IN HEAVEN,
CHOOSE LIFE NOT DEATH. JN17

THE ACCUSER!

THERE IS ONLY ONE ACCUSER THAT WILL CONDEMN YOU, THE
DEVIL. THIS IS EXTREMELY IMPORTANT, YOU CAN SPEAK THE
TRUTH IN LOVE, BUT NEVER ACCUSE OR CONDEMN ANYONE AS

THIS PUTS YOU IN AGREEMENT WITH THE DEVIL AND HE HAS THE LEGAL RIGHT TO BRING YOUR WORDS BACK ON YOU MAT7 EXAMPLE, HOW COULD A CHILD OF AN ALCOHOLIC BECOME AN ALCOHOLIC AFTER EXPERIENCING ALL THAT HORROR, THEY ACCUSE THEIR PARENTS INSTEAD OF PRAYING FOR THEM. THE DEVIL USES THEIR WORDS AND THEY WIND UP LIKE THEIR PARENTS. VERY IMPORTANT, NEVER ACCUSE ANYONE OF ANYTHING. THE DEVIL IS A LIAR, YOU WILL NO LONGER BE A SLAVE TO THE DEVIL'S LIES, SPIRIT OF DEATH, YOU WILL BE FREE FROM THE WORLD AND ALL ITS ADDICTIONS. YAHWEH DID NOT CREATE FEAR, SHAME, GUILT, STRESS, RACISM, BITTERNESS, ANGER, UNFORGIVENESS, HATE, ANXIETY, GREED, PRIDE, AND ANY AND ALL SICKNESS. NONE OF THIS IS REAL, THIS IS ONLY LIES, SPIRIT OF DEATH OF THE DEVIL THAT YOU HAVE AGREED WITH. THE DEVIL CANNOT CREATE ANYTHING, ALL HE CAN DO IS LIE TO YOU AND TRY TO DECEIVE YOU INTO AGREEING WITH HIS LIES, SPIRIT OF DEATH. JN8

JESUS CHRIST – GREAT COMPASSION!

NOW, REALIZE JESUS CHRIST IS GREAT COMPASSION, HE KNEW SICKNESS IS NOT REAL, YAHWEH DID NOT CREATE SICKNESS, SICKNESS IS A DEMONIC SPIRIT, SPIRIT OF DEATH, AND HE CAST IT OUT AND SET THE PEOPLE FREE. BEFORE THE CROSS AND RESURRECTION, JESUS CHRIST WAS ANOINTED WITH THE HOLY SPIRIT AND HEALED ALL THAT WERE OPPRESSED OF THE DEVIL. ACTS 10 SICKNESS IS NOT REAL, IT IS A DEMONIC SPIRIT, SPIRIT OF DEATH THAT JESUS CAST OUT. AFTER THE CROSS AND RESURRECTION, BY JESUS CHRIST'S STRIPES YOU WERE HEALED. 1PETER2 IT IS FINISHED, THE DEVIL IS TOTALLY DEFEATED, THE DEMONIC SPIRIT OF SICKNESS IS TOTALLY DEFEATED. DO NOT

AGREE WITH A DEFEATED DEMONIC SPIRIT, SPIRIT OF DEATH, OR YOU WILL CONTINUE TO PAY THE PRICE THAT JESUS HAS ALREADY PAID IN FULL. LISTEN TO THE COUNSEL OF THE LORD. MAN WILL POISON HIS BODY WITH TOBACCO, ALCOHOL, FOODS, CHEMICALS, FLUORIDE (TOOTH PASTE), ETC. OUT OF HIS OWN MOUTH HE SPEAKS I AM SICK, NOW HE HAS POISONED HIS SOUL. STOP AGREEING WITH THE DEVIL, SPIRIT OF DEATH, STOP POISONING YOUR BODY AND YOUR SOUL. JESUS CHRIST HAS SET ALL MANKIND FREE FROM SIN, SICKNESS, AND DEATH. ALL YOU HAVE TO DO IS AGREE WITH HIM AND RECEIVE ETERNAL LIFE. LATER, I AM ALSO GOING TO TEACH YOU WHICH FOODS RESTORE YOUR IMMUNE SYSTEM IN THE NATURAL, WE WILL APPROACH THE NATURAL AND SUPERNATURAL AND HOW THEY WORK TOGETHER. EXAMPLE, MOST PEOPLE ARE DEHYDRATED AND THEIR SALT LEVEL IS TOO LOW. DRINK ½ YOUR BODY WEIGHT DAILY IN OUNCES OF WATER, 100 LBS./DRINK 50 OUNCES OF WATER AND TAKE ¼ OF TEASPOON OF SEA SALT. THE NATURAL BODY REACTION OF HISTAMINE STOPS AND YOU CAN BREATHE. NEVER FORGET IF YOU FEEL ANY LOSS OF YOUR PEACE, SOMETHING IS AMISS, STOP, CONFESS AND REPENT, TAKE YOUR COMMUNION, SPEAK YOUR TESTIMONY, AND YOUR PEACE WILL RETURN, NATURAL AND SUPERNATURAL WORKING TOGETHER.

JESUS CHRIST: I WILL ALWAYS LOVE YOU!

JESUS CHRIST MAKES IT VERY CLEAR, I LOVE YOU, I WILL ALWAYS LOVE YOU, BUT IF YOU DIE IN YOUR SIN (AGREEMENT WITH THE DEVIL, SPIRIT OF DEATH) THIS MEANS YOU ARE NOT IN AGREEMENT WITH ME, AND IF YOU ARE NOT IN AGREEMENT WITH ME, YOU CANNOT BE WHERE I AM, AND I AM ETERNAL LIFE. JN8 JESUS CHRIST ONLY CAN BLESS YOU WITH YAHWEH'S DNA, SPIRIT OF LIFE, AND YOU BECOME ONE WITH HIM IN ETERNAL LIFE. BELIEVE AND RECEIVE, IN THE TWINKLING OF AN EYE THAT YOU BELIEVE, YOU WILL RECEIVE YAHWEH'S NATURE. **THIS IS**

VERY IMPORTANT, YOU HAVE BEEN CHANGED AND RECEIVED THE NATURE OF GOD. THERE IS NO SIN IN GOD'S NATURE. YOU HAVE BEEN SET FREE FROM THE DEVIL'S NATURE TO SIN. THE HOLY SPIRIT WILL HELP KEEP YOU OUT OF SIN AND IN GOD'S NATURE. YOU DO HAVE FREE WILL SO YOU MUST DO YOUR PART BY DAILY CONFESSING AND REPENTING, TAKING IN COMMUNION, AND SPEAKING YOUR TESTIMONY. THIS KEEPS YOU ONE WITH JESUS SEATED IN HEAVENLY PLACES WITH AUTHORITY OVER THE DEVIL AND OVER ALL SIN. REMEMBER SIN IS AGREEMENT WITH THE SPIRIT OF DEATH. YOU NO LONGER HAVE THAT AGREEMENT. YOU NOW HAVE AN AGREEMENT WITH THE SPIRIT OF ETERNAL LIFE. KEEP YOUR EYES ON JESUS CHRIST, READ AND STUDY HIS LIVING WORD, THE BIBLE, PRAY, TALK TO HIM AND ASK HIM TO REVEAL HIS TRUTH AND WISDOM. YOU WILL NEVER BE THE SAME, YOU WILL BE AN OVERCOMER AND OVERTHROW THE DARKNESS. "LOVE OVERTHROWS THE DARKNESS." 1/18 THS YOU WILL SET THE WORLD ON FIRE WITH THE LIVING WORD AND POWER OF THE TRUTH, THE GOSPEL OF JESUS CHRIST. ACTS2 "A MIRACLE IS SIMPLY THE LIGHT OF THE TRUTH REVEALED, MIRACLES ONLY HAPPEN IN THE PRESENCE OF JESUS CHRIST."2/17 THS PEOPLES LIVES WILL CHANGE RIGHT IN FRONT OF YOUR EYES, HEARTS WILL MELT AND PHYSICAL BODIES HEALED AND RESTORED IN THE UNLIMITED LOVE AND ACCEPTANCE OF JESUS CHRIST.

JESUS CHRIST SET THE SLAVES FREE!

"JESUS CHRIST, ETERNAL LIFE CAME IN THE FLESH TO RESTORE THE ETERNAL LIFE COVENANT, INTIMACY (LOVE AND ACCEPTANCE) BETWEEN YAHWEH, ETERNAL LIFE AND MAN. THE SAME INTIMACY THAT ADAM LOST IN THE GARDEN. ADAM LOST ETERNAL LIFE, ADAM LOST HIS FREEDOM, AND ADAM BECAME A SLAVE. JESUS CHRIST CAME TO DESTROY THE WORKS OF THE DEVIL. 1JN5 JESUS CHRIST SET THE SLAVES FREE, HE RESTORED

ETERNAL LIFE, AND HE RESTORED FREEDOM TO ALL WHO LOVE
AND ACCEPT HIM." 1JN1

LIVING WORD DIVIDING SOUL FROM SPIRIT!

THE LIVING WORD OF YAHWEH IS QUICK AND POWERFUL, AND
SHARPER THAN ANY TWO EDGED SWORD, DIVIDING THE SOUL
FROM THE SPIRIT. WHEN YOU ALLOW THE HOLY SPIRIT TO SPEAK
THROUGH YOU THE LANGUAGE AND VIBRATIONS OF ETERNAL
LIFE, YOU DESTROY THE LIES AND OPPRESSION, SPIRIT OF DEATH,
OFF OF MEN'S SOULS AND SET THEM FREE. HEB4 NOW,
YAHWEH'S SPIRIT IS SPEAKING TO THEIR SPIRIT (SPIRIT TO SPIRIT)
AND REFRESHING AND RESTORATION BEGINS, YAHWEH'S LIVING
WATER REFRESHES THEM TO LIFE AND DESTROYS THE DRYNESS
OF DEATH. THE POWER OF THE WORD OF YAHWEH IS IN THE
SPOKEN WORD, AND HEAVENLY VIBRATIONS. YAHWEH BACKS UP
HIS LIVING WORD THAT COMES OUT OF YOUR MOUTH WITH
SIGNS, WONDERS, AND MIRACLES. MK16

LIFE AND DEATH – TONGUES AND COVENANT!

THE POWER OF LIFE AND DEATH IS IN YOUR WORDS, SPEAK LIFE,
NOT DEATH, AND IN YOUR POWER OF AGREEMENT. WHEN TWO
OR MORE AGREE ON SOMETHING, THIS BECOMES A COVENANT
BETWEEN THEM. MAT18 JESUS CHRIST CAME IN THE FLESH TO
EARTH, HE IS ETERNAL LIFE, AND HE BROUGHT WITH HIM THE
ETERNAL LIFE COVENANT. FATHER YAHWEH,
JESUS CHRIST, AND THE HOLY SPIRIT, ALL AGREE ON ETERNAL
LIFE, AND THIS FORMS THE ETERNAL LIFE COVENANT. 1JN5.
WHEN YOU AGREE WITH JESUS CHRIST, YOU BECOME PART OF
THE ETERNAL LIFE COVENANT ON EARTH AS IT IS IN HEAVEN.
MAT6

PERSONAL TESTIMONY!

PRAISE GOD, I AM VERY HEALTHY, I EAT RIGHT, DRINK ONLY WATER, AND EXERCISE REGULARLY. I CONFESS, REPENT, AND TAKE COMMUNION OFTEN. I TAKE NO PRESCRIPTION DRUGS OF ANY KIND, AND MY BLOOD PRESSURE RUNS 110 OVER 68. WHEN NEW YORK PASSED THE ABORTION BILL AND THE BABY COULD BE MURDERED UP UNTIL THE DAY BEFORE IT WAS DUE, ALL HELL BROKE LOOSE. THE SPIRT OF GOD, THE HOLY SPIRIT, REVEALED TO ME THAT THE #1 HENCHMAN OF THE SPIRIT OF DEATH WAS RELEASED ACROSS THE EAST COAST. THIS SPIRIT OF DEATH WAS RELEASED BY MAN, AND THIS SPIRIT WOULD GO AFTER EVERYONE, ESPECIALLY YOUNG FEMALES OF CHILD BEARING AGE. DEATH EXPLODED, THE STATE OF VIRGINIA, WAS READY TO MURDER THE BABY AFTER IT WAS BORN AND OTHER STATES STARTED FOLLOWING AFTER NY AND VA. THE HOLY SPIRIT HAD ME PUT OUT THE WARNING TO BE ON GUARD.

NOW, HERE IS WHAT HAPPENED TO ME. A FEW DAYS AFTER THIS REVELATION, I WOKE UP AT 2 AM, AND MY RIGHT SIDE WOULD NOT FUNCTION PROPERLY. I HALF WAY CRAWLED INTO THE BATHROOM, MY RIGHT SIDE WOULD NOT WORK, I COULD NOT GET MY RIGHT HAND TO FUNCTION. I TRIED TO GET SOME WATER TO DRINK AND I COULD NOT DO IT. IN THE NATURAL, THE PERFECT STORM FOR A STROKE. THE HOLY SPIRIT BROUGHT ME TO MY SENSES, AND OPENED MY EYES TO WHAT IS REAL AND NOT REAL. I SPOKE THIS IS NOT REAL, AND I DO NOT AGREE WITH IT, BY JESUS CHRIST'S STRIPES I WAS HEALED. I CONFESSED, REPENTED, AND STARTED SPEAKING IN THE LANGUAGE OF ETERNAL LIFE, TONGUES, AND I BEGAN INTENSE SPIRITUAL WARFARE. IN A SHORT AMOUNT OF TIME I WAS ALMOST

NORMAL, I COULD NOW TAKE COMMUNION. I WENT BACK TO
BED, STILL EXPERIENCING SOME SYMPTOMS. I CONTINUED
PRAYING IN THE LANGUAGE OF THE SPIRIT OF LIFE, UNTIL I WENT
TO SLEEP. PRAISE GOD, I WOKE UP THE NEXT MORNING TOTALLY
HEALTHY, AS IF IT NEVER HAPPENED. BECAUSE IT DID NOT, IT
WAS A LIE FROM HELL THAT I DID NOT AGREE WITH, OR BELIEVE.
THEN THE HOLY SPIRIT REMINDED ME OF THE SCRIPTURE ABOUT
THE ELECT BEING DECEIVED. HE REVEALED THAT MANY OF THE
ELECT WOULD BE ATTACKED IN SIMILAR FASHION, AND RATHER
THAN STANDING FIRM, THEY WOULD GIVE IN TO WHAT IS NOT
REAL, BECAUSE THEY HAD NOT BEEN TAUGHT HOW TO DO
SPIRITUAL WARFARE. HE THEN INSTRUCTED ME TO TEACH THEM
SPIRITUAL WARFARE BOTH IN WORDS AND ACTION. IN MY CASE
A LOT OF PEOPLE WOULD HAVE AGREED WITH THE LIE, THAT
THEY WERE HAVING A STROKE. NEXT, THE AMBULANCE RIDE TO
THE HOSPITAL EMERGENCY ROOM, HOOKED UP TO DRUGS,
SPEND SEVERAL DAYS IN THE HOSPITAL, AND THEN SENT HOME
TO BE ON SOME KIND OF DRUGS FOR THE REST OF THEIR LIFE,
SLAVES TO THE PHARMACEUTICAL INDUSTRY. ALL OF THIS FOR
SOMETHING THAT IS NOT REAL. PLEASE PAY CLOSE ATTENTION
TO THIS MANUAL AND LEARN HOW TO BE A TRUE EMPOWERED
SON OF GOD, AND YOU WILL NEVER BE A SLAVE TO THE SPIRIT OF
DEATH, YOU WILL BE AN OVERCOMER.

THE HOLY SPIRIT DIRECTED ME TO CLEAR UP TWO MORE
MISUNDERSTANDINGS IN THE CHURCH. GOD IS A GOD OF
ORDER, NOT CONFUSION. 1ST COR 14. #1 – WE ARE THE BODY OF
CHRIST, EPH. 4, NOT THE BRIDE OF CHRIST. REV. 21. #2 – THERE
WILL NOT BE A ONE WORLD ORDER, REV. 6, UNTIL JESUS CHRIST
RETURNS AND SETS UP *HIS* KINGDOM. REV. 20. ALL OF THE

ANSWERS YOU SEEK ARE FOUND IN THE HOLY LIVING WORD OF GOD, THE GOD BREATHED HOLY BIBLE.

NOW, PREPARE YOURSELF TO BELIEVE AND RECEIVE THE SEVEN STEPS TO THE WISDOM OF YAHWEH, THE KNOWLEDGE OF JESUS CHRIST.

SEVEN STEPS OF WISDOM TO BELIEVE AND RECEIVE ETERNAL LIFE!

1. ASK THE HOLY SPIRIT, THE SPIRIT OF JESUS CHRIST, TO REVEAL JESUS CHRIST TO YOU, SURRENDER YOUR ALL TO JESUS CHRIST, YOU ARE A SINNER IN AGREEMENT WITH THE DEVIL, CONFESS, REPENT OF YOUR SIN, AGREEMENT WITH THE SPIRIT OF DEATH, AND ASK AND RECEIVE BY FAITH, (TRUSTING, OBEYING, AND ACTING ON YAHWEH'S HOLY LIVING WORD OF TRUTH), JESUS CHRIST TO FORGIVE YOU OF YOUR SIN.

2. YOU ASK AND RECEIVE BY FAITH JESUS CHRIST TO COME AND LIVE INSIDE YOU, BLESSING YOU BY MAKING HIS HOME IN YOU, TO CHANGE YOUR MIND AND YOUR HEART TO BE LIKE HIS MIND AND HIS HEART, PROCLAIM HIM FROM YOUR LIPS AS YOUR LORD AND SAVIOUR AND THANK FATHER YAHWEH

FOR RAISING HIM FROM THE DEAD BY HIS HOLY SPIRIT POWER.

3. YOU ARE BAPTIZED IN WATER, THIS BECOMES THE PRECIOUS BLOOD OF JESUS CHRIST IN THE SPIRIT REALM, AND WASHES AWAY THE SPIRIT OF DEATH. YOU ARE BAPTIZED IN THE NAME OF FATHER GOD , JESUS CHRIST, AND THE HOLY SPIRIT FOR REPENTENCE, TURNING AWAY FROM YOUR SIN, AND YOUR AGREEMENT WITH THE SPIRIT OF DEATH. YOU NOW HAVE A NEW BEGINNING, A NEW BIRTH. YOU ARE A NEW CREATURE NOW BECOMING ONE WITH JESUS CHRIST IN NEW LIFE, NOT DEATH. THIS FULFILLS ALL RIGHTEOUSNESS.

4. YOU ASK AND RECEIVE BY FAITH THE PRECIOUS BLOOD OF JESUS CHRIST TO FORGIVE AND WASH AWAY ALL YOUR SIN, WASH AWAY THE SPIRIT OF DEATH. YOU ARE NOW CLEANSED AND SET FREE FROM ALL OPPRESSION, SPIRIT OF DEATH OF THE DEVIL.

5. YOU ASK AND RECEIVE BY FAITH TO BE BORN AGAIN IN YAHWEH'S HOLY SPIRIT. JUST LIKE JESUS CHRIST THE HOLY SPIRIT IS NOW YOUR FATHER, YOU ARE BORN AGAIN IN THE SPIRIT, NOW BOTH BY WATER AND THE

SPIRIT. YOU ARE NOW A NEW CREATION IN THE
FAMILY OF YAHWEH, YOU ARE TRANSLATED OUT OF
DARKNESS INTO HIS MARVELOUS LIGHT.

6. YOU ASK AND RECEIVE BY FAITH JESUS CHRIST TO
    BAPTIZE YOU, (YOUR SOUL AND SPIRIT ARE BAPTIZED
    INTO YAHWEH'S SOUL AND SPIRIT), BLESSING YOU BY
    MAKING YOU HIS HOME AND ENDUE YOU WITH HIS
    POWER AND FIRE (THE HOLY SPIRIT) AND BLESS YOU
    WITH YAHWEH'S DNA, SPIRIT OF LIFE, TO MANIFEST
    HIS HOLY RIGHTEOUSNESS, TO BECOME HIS WITNESS
    IN ALL THE EARTH, TO SPEAK FORTH IN THE
    LANGUAGE AND VIBRATIONS OF ETERNAL LIFE, TO LIFT
    PEOPLE UP INTO HIS PRESENCE AND OPERATE IN HIS
    MIRACLES OF RESTORATION, SPIRIT, SOUL, AND BODY,
    TO SET PEOPLE FREE FROM ALL THE LIES AND
    OPPRESSION, SPIRIT OF DEATH OF THE DEVIL.

7. HALLELUJAH, YOU ARE NOW IN TOTAL AGREEMENT
    WITH JESUS CHRIST IN THE ETERNAL
    LIFE COVENANT. PROCLAIM, I AM A SON OF YAHWEH,
    LOVED AND ACCEPTED WITH ETERNAL LIFE. NOW
    SEAL YOU'RE YOUR ETERNAL LIFE COVENANT BY
    HAVING COMMUNION, BECOMING ONE WITH JESUS
    CHRIST BY TAKING IN HIS BODY AND BLOOD, A FRESH
    TRANSFUSION OF HIS DNA, SPIRIT OF ETERNAL LIFE,
    THIS LIFTS YOU UP INTO HIS PRESENCE, INTIMACY,
    TRUE SONSHIP. THIS SEATS YOU IN HEAVENLY PLACES

WITH AUTHORITY OVER THE DEVIL AND ANYTHING TO
DO WITH DEATH. NOW YOU CAN SEE WHAT IS REAL
AND WHAT IS NOT REAL, WHAT IS TRUE AND WHAT IS
NOT TRUE, AND THE TRUTH WILL SET YOU FREE. YOU
WILL BEGIN TO SEE AS JESUS CHRIST SEES, STOP
BELIEVING WHAT YOU SEE, SEE, WHAT YOU BELIEVE
AS JESUS CHRIST SEES. "AS HE IS, SO ARE WE IN THIS
WORLD". 1ST JOHN 4

JESUS CHRIST IS ETERNAL LIFE, WE ARE ETERNAL LIFE
ON THIS EARTH AS HE IS IN HEAVEN. 1ST JN 5

JESUS CHRIST'S PROCLAMATION!

NOW BOLDLY PROCLAIM WHAT JESUS CHRIST PROCLAIMED
"THE SPIRIT OF THE LORD IS UPON ME, BECAUSE HE HATH
ANOINTED ME TO PREACH THE GOSPEL TO THE POOR; HE
HATH SENT ME TO HEAL THE BROKEN HEARTED, TO PREACH
DELIVERANCE TO THE CAPTIVES, AND RECOVERING OF
SIGHT TO THE BLIND, TO SET AT LIBERTY THEM THAT ARE
BRUISED. TO PREACH THE ACCEPTABLE YEAR OF THE
LORD."LUKE4
JESUS CHRIST ALSO PROCLAIMED: "VERILY, VERILY, I SAY
UNTO YOU, HE THAT BELIEVETH ON ME, THE WORKS THAT I
DO SHALL HE DO ALSO; AND GREATER WORKS THAN THESE
SHALL HE DO; BECAUSE I GO UNTO MY FATHER." JN14 AND
BECAUSE I GO UNTO MY FATHER, I WILL NOT LEAVE YOU
COMFORTLESS, I WILL SEND THE HOLY SPIRIT TO LIVE INSIDE
YOU, BLESSING YOU BY MAKING YOU HIS HOME, HIS
SANCTUARY, HIS CHURCH, HIS HOLINESS IS NOW YOUR
HOLINESS, ENDUE YOU WITH HIS POWER TO DO THE

GREATER WORKS OF TRUE SONS AND DAUGHTERS OF YAHWEH. JN 16 HOME IS A PLACE FILLED WITH LOVE, PEACE, AND JOY. THE HOLY SPIRIT IS AT HOME IN YOU, A PLACE WHERE YOU WANT TO BE, HE IS NOT A GUEST, HE IS FAMILY. HE IS GENTLE AND PEACEFUL AND WILL NEVER FORCE YOU TO DO ANYTHING THAT YOU ARE UNCOMFORTABLE WITH. HE IS THE COMFORTER, BUT HE IS ALSO YAHWEH, AND IF YOU WILL ALLOW HIM, HE WILL USE YOU, TO USE A MILITARY TERM, A COMMAND BASE OF OPERATIONS TO WORK FROM AND THROUGH TO DESTROY THE WORKS OF THE DEVIL. AND WITH YOUR PERMISSION AND ENTHUSIASM YOU ARE NOW A SOLDIER OF JESUS CHRIST, IN HIS ARMY TO USE AND BRING FORTH HIS OBJECTIVE, ETERNAL LIFE FOR ALL MANKIND. YOU ARE NOW A TRUE EMISSARY OF JESUS CHRIST.

JESUS CHRIST: KEY TO ABIDING IN HIS PRESENCE!

THE KEY TO STAYING IN AGREEMENT WITH JESUS CHRIST, ABIDING IN HIS PRESENCE, AND OPERATING IN HIS MIRACLES OF LOVE, IS THE FOLLOWING....

DAILY:

A) READ YOUR BIBLE, TRUST, OBEY AND ACT ON YAHWEH'S HOLY LIVING WORD OF TRUTH.

B) CONFESS AND REPENT: JESUS CHRIST, I CONFESS AND REPENT OF MY SIN (AGREEMENT WITH THE DEVIL, SPIRIT OF DEATH), THAT WOULD KEEP YOU FROM ABIDING IN ME AND ME FROM ABIDING IN YOU. HOLY SPIRIT, JESUS CHRIST, FATHER YAHWEH CLEANSE ME FROM ALL UNRIGHTEOUSNESS, SET ME FREE, GIVE ME YOUR PEACE, LIFT ME INTO YOUR PRESENCE, INTO YOUR MARVELOUS LIGHT, INTO ETERNAL LIFE ON EARTH AS IT IS IN HEAVEN, THE SAME LOVE THAT CREATED ME IS RESTORING ME NOW, RESTORATION OF ALL IN ALL AS IF IT NEVER HAPPENED. I BELIEVE IT AND I RECEIVE IT AND I THANK JESUS CHRIST FOR IT.

C) TAKE COMMUNION: TO BECOME ONE WITH JESUS CHRIST, TAKING IN HIS BODY AND BLOOD, A FRESH TRANSFUSION OF JESUS CHRIST'S DNA, SPIRIT OF ETERNAL LIFE, OVERCOMES THE SPIRIT OF DEATH, LIFTS YOU UP INTO HIS PRESENCE, SEATS YOU IN HEAVENLY PLACES, INTIMATE SONSHIP. JESUS CHRIST SAID MY BODY AND MY BLOOD ARE TRUE FOOD INDEED, SO ANY FOOD AND ANY LIQUID CAN BE USED. THIS WAY YOU CAN HAVE COMMUNION BEFORE EVERY MEAL, THIS IS ALSO FIRST FRUITS TO HIM. ASK HIM TO FILL YOU WITH HE SPIRIT OF LIFE. THANK HIM FOR ETERNAL LIFE.

TESTIMONY: "I AM A NEW CREATURE FILLED WITH THE HOLY SPIRIT OF ALMIGHTY GOD, THE SPIRIT OF ETERNAL LIFE, SEATED IN HEAVENLY PLACES WITH JESUS CHRIST, MY LORD AND SAVIOR. I AM NOT SUBJECT TO NATURAL LAW, NATURAL LAW IS SUBJECT TO ME. I AM NOT OF THIS WORLD, **I HAVE AUTHORITY OVER DEATH, *DEATH HAS NO HOLD ON ME***. I AM A TRUE SON OR DAUGHTER OF GOD, MADE IN THE IMAGE OF GOD, LOVED, ACCEPTED, AND RESTORED WITH ETERNAL LIFE ON EARTH AS IT IS IN HEAVEN. I AM GOING TO LIVE ON THIS EARTH HEALTHY, WHOLE, PROSPEROUS, BLESSED, REGENERATED AND RESTORED, IN LOVE, PEACE, AND JOY, SPIRIT, SOUL AND BODY BLAMELESS, UNTIL JESUS RETURNS. AND HE WILL FIND ME SOWING THE SPIRIT OF LIFE, JESUS CHRIST THE ANSWER ETERNAL LIFE INTO ALL THE WORLD, AND SETTING FREE ALL OF CREATION FROM THE SPIRIT OF DEATH, AND THEN I AM GOING TO LIVE, RULE AND REIGN WITH HIM FOREVER. THANK YOU JESUS FOR SETTING ME FREE! AMEN!"

NOW, JOIN JESUS CHRIST'S REVOLUTION, LOVE THEM INTO THE KINGDOM, BE GENTLE, SPEAK THE TRUTH, ALLOW THE HOLY SPIRIT TO SPEAK THROUGH YOU THE LANGUAGE AND VIBRATIONS OF ETERNAL LIFE. PROCEED FORCEFULLY WITH SPIRITUAL WARFARE, DESTROY THE LIES OF THE DEVIL, OVERCOME THE SPIRIT OF DEATH, LAY HANDS ON THE SICK AND WATCH THEM RECOVER, OPERATE IN HIS MIRACLES AND SET MANKIND FREE TO ETERNAL LIFE. REMEMBER THE WORDS OF JESUS CHRIST "I AM COMING." I AM LIFE, LOVE, PEACE, AND JOY.

JESUS CHRIST: INTENSE SPIRITUAL WARFARE!

NOW, FOR THOSE OF YOU THAT ARE READY TO GO INTO THE DEEPER TRUTHS OF YAHWEH, I AM GOING TO TEACH YOU SERIOUS SPIRITUAL WARFARE. FIRST, YOU MUST ALWAYS ASK PERMISSION, TO PRAY FOR AND TO LAY HANDS ON PEOPLE, UNDERSTAND ANY FORM OF MANIPULATION IS WITCHCRAFT, SPIRIT OF DEATH. IF THEY HAVE COME TO YOU FOR PRAYER, THIS IS UNDERSTOOD. REALIZE, LAYING ON OF HANDS, TRANSFERS THE ANOINTING OF THE HOLY SPIRIT, THE ANOINTING IS TANGIBLE. NEXT, BEFORE YOU MINISTER TO SOMEONE ALWAYS CONFESS AND REPENT SO THAT YOU ARE CLEANSED AND THE POWER OF YAHWEH CAN FLOW THROUGH YOU TO DESTROY THE WORKS OF THE DEVIL AND RESTORE THEM ALL IN ALL. NOW, YOU MUST REALIZE WHO YOU ARE AND THE POWER AND AUTHORITY THAT YOU HAVE BEEN GIVEN. ALL THINGS ARE POSSIBLE WITH JESUS CHRIST. LK 18 HEAR THE WORDS OF JESUS CHRIST "IF YOU HAVE FAITH AS A GRAIN OF MUSTARD SEED, YOU SHALL SAY UNTO THIS MOUNTAIN, REMOVE HENCE TO YONDER PLACE AND IT SHALL REMOVE, AND NOTHING SHALL BE IMPOSSIBLE UNTO YOU. HALLELUJAH, THIS MEANS FOR THOSE IN JESUS CHRIST WITH HIS DNA, SPIRIT OF ETERNAL LIFE, AND ENDUED WITH THE POWER OF THE HOLY SPIRIT, ALL THINGS ARE POSSIBLE. M17 YOU NOW HAVE THE DOMINION POWER THAT ADAM HAD IN THE GARDEN BEFORE THE FALL. THS AGAIN, LISTEN TO THE WORDS OF JESUS CHRIST, "AND WHATSOEVER YOU SHALL ASK IN MY NAME, THAT I WILL DO, THAT MY FATHER MAY BE GLORIFIED IN THE SON. IF YOU SHALL ASK ANYTHING IN MY NAME I WILL DO IT. JN 14 GLORY TO YAHWEH, JESUS CHRIST JUST GAVE US HIS POWER OF ATTORNEY. WE NOW KNOW THAT ALL THINGS ARE POSSIBLE AND WE HAVE HIS POWER OF ATTORNEY TO USE HIS NAME AND BRING IT FORTH. JESUS CHRIST WENT ON TO SAY "I BEHELD SATAN AS LIGHTNING FALL FROM HEAVEN. BEHOLD I GIVE UNTO YOU POWER TO TREAD ON SERPENTS AND SCORPIONS AND OVER

LL THE POWER OF THE ENEMY, AND NOTHING SHALL BY ANY MEANS HURT YOU. YOU ARE SEATED IN HEAVENLY PLACES WITH JESUS CHRIST AND YOU HAVE AUTHORITY OVER THE DEVIL, THE SPIRIT OF DEATH. REMEMBER, THE DEVIL IS A CREATED BEING AND THROUGH JESUS CHRIST YOU HAVE AUTHORITY OVER ALL CREATION, THIS INCLUDES ANYTHING THAT DEALS WITH DEATH SUCH AS SICKNESS, DISEASE, AGING, POVERTY, ETC. LK10 JESUS CHRIST HAS ALSO GIVEN TO YOU NUMEROUS TOOLS TO WORK WITH. SOME OF THESE INCLUDE COMMUNION, ALLOWING THE HOLY SPIRIT TO SPEAK THROUGH YOU THE LANGUAGE AND VIBRATIONS OF ETERNAL LIFE, ANOINTING OIL, PRAISE AND WORSHIP MUSIC, AND THE SHOFAR. WHEN WE BLOW THE SHOFAR AND ALLOW THE HOLY SPIRIT TO SPEAK THROUGH US THE LANGUAGE OF ETERNAL LIFE, THE FREQUENCY OF HEAVEN IS RELEASED AND THE POWER AND LIGHT OF THE HOLY SPIRIT IS RELEASED AND THIS DESTROYS THE OPPRESSION, SPIRIT OF DEATH, OF THE DEVIL, DOWN TO THE CELLULAR LEVEL AND DESTROYS THE DEVIL'S DNA, SPIRIT OF ETERNAL DEATH. RESTORATION BEGINS AS THEY BREATHE IN THE HOLY SPIRIT, AND HE IS CARRIED BY THE BLOOD TO ALL PARTS OF THE BODY. PRAISE AND WORSHIP MUSIC IN HEAVEN'S FREQUENCY ACCELERATES RESTORATION. ANOINTING OIL BLESSES AND SETS YOU APART FOR YAHWEH. COMMUNION, WASHES AWAY ALL YOUR SIN, WASHES AWAY SPIRIT OF DEATH, A FRESH TRANSFUSION OF JESUS CHRIST'S DNA, SPIRIT OF ETERNAL LIFE, AGAIN DESTROYING ALL OF THE OPPRESSION, SPIRIT OF DEATH OF THE DEVIL, DOWN TO THE CELLULAR LEVEL, DESTROYS THE DEVIL'S DNA, SPIRIT OF ETERNAL DEATH. ALL OF THESE LIFT YOU UP INTO HIS PRESENCE, SEATS YOU IN HEAVENLY PLACES WHERE THE MIRACLES TAKE PLACE. REMEMBER, SIN IS YOUR AGREEMENT WITH THE DEVIL, THE SPIRIT OF ETERNAL DEATH. THIS IS VERY IMPORTANT FOR YOU TO UNDERSTAND. THE OPPRESSION, SPIRIT OF DEATH, BLINDNESS OF THE DEVIL, MUST BE BROKEN AND REMOVED OFF OF PEOPLE SO THAT THEY CAN BE

SET FREE, SEE, AND HEAR THE TRUTH OF JESUS CHRIST. THIS
PROCESS BEGINS BY CONFESSING AND REPENTING, TAKING
COMMUNION, LAYING ON OF HANDS, AND SPEAKING IN THE
LANGUAGE OF ETERNAL LIFE. JESUS CHRIST SAID USE MY NAME,
THIS IS WHERE THE POWER AND AUTHORITY TO BIND AND LOOSE
ORIGINATES FROM. YOU SPEAK FORTH IN THE NAME OF JESUS
CHRIST, DEVIL, JESUS CHRIST REBUKE YOU, JESUS CHRIST BIND
YOU, JESUS CHRIST CAST YOU OUT. THIS IS HOW YAHWEH USES
YOU TO SPEAK FORTH IN HIS POWER AND AUTHORITY TO
DESTROY ALL OPPRESSION OF THE DEVIL AND HIS MINIONS.
NEVER SAY I REBUKE, OR I BIND OR I CAST OUT AS THIS PUTS YOU
IN AGREEMENT WITH THE DEVIL, AND HE LAUGHS AT YOU AS HE
TAKES YOU DEEPER INTO HIS DARKNESS OF LIES. HOWEVER, YOU
DO HAVE THE POWER AND AUTHORITY TO CANCEL ANY AND ALL
AGREEMENTS THAT YOU HAVE MADE OR THAT ANYONE ELSE HAS
MADE FOR AND AGAINST YOU WITH THE DEVIL. YOU CAN ALSO
CANCEL ANY WORDS SPOKEN AGAINST YOU, BY SIMPLY SAYING
DO NOT AGREE WITH WHAT YOU SAID AND I CANCEL YOUR
WORDS IN JESUS CHRIST'S NAME.
THESE ARE THE WORDS FOR YOU TO SPEAK FORTH AND HAVE
OTHERS REPEAT AFTER YOU:

IN THE NAME OF JESUS CHRIST, THE ANSWER, ETERNAL LIFE, AND
HIS PRECIOUS BLOOD, BY THE POWER OF THE HOLY SPIRIT, DEVIL
SPIRIT OF DEATH, JESUS CHRIST REBUKE YOU, JESUS CHRIST BIND
YOU, AND JESUS CHRIST CAST YOU OUT. AND I CANCEL ANY AND
ALL AGREEMENTS THAT I HAVE MADE WITH YOU, KNOWINGLY
AND UNKNOWINGLY. AND I CANCEL ANY AND ALL AGREEMENTS
THAT ANYONE ELSE HAS MADE FOR ME WITH YOU SINCE AND
BEFORE MY BEGINNING AND UP AND UNTIL NOW. I WILLINGLY
RECEIVE JESUS CHRIST AS MY LORD AND SAVIOR, JESUS CHRIST
BAPTIZE ME WITH YOUR HOLY SPIRIT, MAKE ME YOUR HOME,
AND BLESS ME WITH YOUR DNA, SPIRIT OF ETERNAL LIFE,
EMPOWER ME TO MANIFEST YOUR HOLY RIGHTEOUSNESS, TO

SPEAK FORTH IN THE LANGUAGE OF ETERNAL LIFE, RESTORATION
OF ALL IN ALL AS IF IT NEVER HAPPENED. I AGREE AND THANK
YOU JESUS CHRIST FOR THE GIFT OF ETERNAL LIFE ON EARTH AS
IT IS IN HEAVEN. I AM A SON OF YAHWEH, LOVED AND
ACCEPTED, WITH ETERNAL LIFE. I CHOOSE LIFE NOT DEATH. I
BELIEVE IT AND I RECEIVE IT AND I THANK JESUS CHRIST FOR IT.

HALLELUJAH, TOGETHER WITH GOD AND HIS POWER YOU HAVE
BROKEN AND CAST OUT THE DEVIL, SPIRIT OF DEATH, AND ALL
HIS MINIONS. YOU HAVE DESTROYED ALL THE WITCHCRAFT,
SPIRIT OF DEATH, _USED_ AGAINST YOU, AND THE PEOPLE THAT
YOU ARE MINISTERING TO. NOW, THEY CAN BELIEVE AND
RECEIVE WHAT YAHWEH HAS FOR THEM, ETERNAL LIFE ON EARTH
AS IT IS IN HEAVEN.

SIMPLICITY OF LIFE!

NOW LISTEN CLOSELY TO HOW SIMPLE THE FULLNESS OF LIFE
CAN BE. JESUS CHRIST IS THE SOURCE OF ALL LIFE, THE SPIRIT OF
LIFE, ETERNAL LIFE. THE DEVIL, SIN, IS THE SPIRIT OF DEATH,
ETERNAL DEATH. FIRST YOU RECEIVE JESUS CHRIST AS YOUR
LORD AND SAVIOR, AND BECOME ONE WITH HIM. YOU ARE
BAPTIZED AND ALL YOUR SIN, SPIRIT OF DEATH IS WASHED AWAY.
YOU ARE NOW CLEANSED OF ALL UNRIGHTOUSNESS, SET FREE,
HAVE HIS PEACE, LIFTED INTO HIS PRESENCE, SEATED IN
HEAVENLY PLACES, INTO THE SPIRIT OF LIFE, ETERNAL LIFE. YOU
ARE NOW IN LIFE, BUT YOU SIN, YOU GET INTO AGREEMENT
WITH THE DEVIL, THE SPIRIT OF DEATH. YOU ARE NOW BACK IN
DEATH, BUT JESUS CHRIST MADE A WAY WHERE THERE WAS NO
WAY. YOU CONFESS AND REPENT OF YOUR SIN, AGREEMENT
WITH THE DEVIL, AGREEMENT WITH THE SPIRIT OF DEATH, TAKE

COMMUNION, THIS WASHES AWAY THE SPIRIT OF DEATH AND YOU ARE SET FREE AGAIN. TAKE COMMUNION A MINIMUM OF FOUR TIMES PER DAY, BREAKFAST, LUNCH, DINNER, AND BEFORE YOU GO TO BED. NOW I KNOW WHY THE HOLY SPIRIT TOLD ME TO TAKE COMMUNION EVERY HOUR ON THE HOUR. THE MORE YOU STAY IN LIFE, THE PRESENCE OF JESUS CHRIST, THE STRONGER AND HEALTHIER YOU BECOME. YOUR SPIRIT SOARS, YOUR SOUL IS AT PEACE AND YOUR PHYSICAL BODY RESTORES FASTER AND ACTUALLY REGENERATES AND YOU BECOME YOUNGER, THE FOUNTAIN OF YOUTH. HALLELUJAH, YOU NOW HAVE THE SECRET OF LIFE, IN JESUS CHRIST, ETERNAL LIFE ON EARTH AS IT IS IN HEAVEN. PREACH IT FROM THE ROOF TOPS, SHARE THIS REVELATION WITH EVERYONE YOU KNOW, AND EVERYONE YOU MEET.

A) INTIMACY: LIFE, LOVE AND ACCEPTANCE "ETERNAL LIFE"

B) COVENANT: WHEN TWO OR MORE AGREE

C) FAITH: AGREEMENT WITH JESUS CHRIST. AGREEMENT WITH THE SPIRIT OF LIFE, ETERNAL LIFE. BELIEVING AND RECEIVING, TRUSTING, OBEYING AND ACTING ON YAHWEH'S HOLY LIVING WORD OF TRUTH. THE INSTANT THAT YOU BELIEVE YOU RECEIVE YAHWEH'S NATURE.

D) SIN: AGREEMENT WITH THE DEVIL. AGREEMENT WITH THE SPIRIT OF DEATH, ETERNAL DEATH.

E) SOUL: YOUR MIND, YOUR WILL AND YOUR EMOTIONS.

F) NEW BIRTH: BAPTISM BY WATER IN THE NAME OF YAHWEH, JESUS CHRIST, AND THE HOLY SPIRIT, BY THE BLOOD OF JESUS CHRIST, ALL SINS WASHED AWAY, SPIRIT OF DEATH WASHED AWAY, AND BORN AGAIN IN THE HOLY SPIRIT, BLESSING YOU BY MAKING YOUR BODY HIS HOME.

G) BAPTISM OF THE HOLY SPIRIT: JESUS CHRIST BAPTIZES YOUR SOUL AND SPIRIT INTO HIS SOUL AND SPIRIT, BLESSING YOU BY MAKING YOU HIS HOME AND COMMAND BASE OF OPERATIONS. HE ENDUES YOU WITH HIS POWER AND FIRE, THE HOLY SPIRIT AND BLESSES YOU WITH HIS DNA, SPIRIT OF ETERNAL LIFE, TO MANIFEST HIS HOLY RIGHTEOUSNESS, TO BECOME HIS WITNESS IN ALL THE EARTH, TO SPEAK FORTH IN HIS LANGUAGE AND VIBRATIONS OF ETERNAL LIFE, TO LIFT PEOPLE UP INTO HIS PRESENCE AND OPERATE IN HIS MIRACLES OF RESTORATION, SPIRIT, SOUL, AND BODY.

H) COMMUNION: TO BECOME ONE WITH JESUS CHRIST BY TAKING IN HIS BODY AND BLOOD, A FRESH TRANSFUSION OF HIS DNA, SPIRIT OF ETERNAL LIFE, ALL YOUR SIN, SPIRIT OF DEATH, WASHED AWAY LIFTS YOU UP INTO HIS PRESENCE, SEATS YOU IN HEAVENLY PLACES, INTIMACY, LOVE AND ACCEPTANCE, TRUE SONSHIP IN THE ETERNAL LIFE COVENANT.

I) ETERNAL LIFE COVENANT: FATHER YAHWEH, JESUS CHRIST, AND HIS HOLY SPIRIT ALL AGREE ON ETERNAL LIFE. WHEN YOU AGREE WITH THEM, YOU NOW HAVE AN ETERNAL LIFE COVENANT WITH YAHWEH. YOU ARE NO LONGER A SLAVE, YOU ARE SET FREE FROM THE WORLD AND ALL OF ITS ADDICTIONS, SET FREE FROM ALL OPPRESSION OF THE DEVIL.

J) PRAISE: THANKING YAHWEH FOR WHAT HE HAS DONE AND WHAT HE IS DOING AND HIS REWARD OF FAITH, THE GIFT OF ETERNAL LIFE, THROUGH JESUS CHRIST.

K) WORSHIP: THANKING YAHWEH FOR WHO HE IS AND WHO WE ARE IN HIM, TRUE SONS AND DAUGHTERS FOLLOWING JESUS CHRIST TO WORSHIP IN SPIRIT AND IN TRUTH.

L) THE HOLY SPIRIT: YAHWEH, THE BREATH AND SPIRIT OF JESUS CHRIST, THE GIVER OF LIFE, THE SPIRIT OF ETERNAL LIFE.

M) GOD'S DNA – SPIRIT OF LIFE, ETERNAL LIFE

N) DEVIL'S DNA – SPIRIT OF DEATH, ETERNAL DEATH.

BLESSING,

JOIN JESUS CHRIST'S REVOLUTION OF LIFE, LOVE AND ACCEPTANCE

JESUS CHRIST THE ANSWER ETERNAL LIFE,

LIFE, LOVE, PEACE, AND JOY,

PASTOR JAMES M. HEATON III

JANUARY 2020

ETERNALLIFECOVENANT.COM

CHOOSELIFENOTDEATH.COM

THS: REVELATIONS OF THE HOLY SPIRIT GIVEN TO PASTOR JAME

IN SUMMARY

WE HAVE ALLOWED THE SPIRIT OF DEATH A FOOTHOLD IN OUR CULTURE. OUR CHILDREN ARE BOMBARDED CONSTANTLY WITH THE SPIRIT OF DEATH. IT REALLY IS QUITE SIMPLE, ANY TIME JESUS CHRIST, THE SPIRIT OF LIFE, SOURCE OF ALL LIFE, ETERNAL LIFE IS REMOVED, THE DEVIL, THE SPIRIT OF DEATH MOVES IN. WE HAVE ALLOWED POLITICS, MEDIA, TV, RADIO, NEWS PRINT, SOCIAL MEDIA, SCHOOL SYSTEMS, ETC. TO REMOVE JESUS CHRIST AND HIS TRUTH. OUR CHILDREN AND ADULTS ARE CONFUSED WITH ALL OF THIS DEATH, AND NOW A NUMBER OF CHURCHES ARE EMBRACING THE SPIRIT OF DEATH, AGREEING WITH ABORTION, HOMOSEXUALITY, AND OTHER PERVERSIONS. OUR CHILDREN DESPERATELY NEED THE TRUTH, AND A WAY TO HEAR THE TRUTH. THEY NEED TO KNOW THAT THERE IS MORE THAN A WAY OUT, BUT HOW TO BE OVERCOMERS, TO BE TRUE SONS AND DAUGHTERS OF GOD, WITH ALL THE PROMISES OF GOD, AND KNOW THAT THEY HAVE ETERNAL LIFE NOW ON EARTH AS IT IS IN HEAVEN. THAT JESUS CHRIST IS IN TOTAL CONTROL, THE DEVIL, SPIRIT OF DEATH IS DEFEATED AND THEY BELONG TO THE CREATOR, SOURCE OF ALL LIFE, LOVE, PEACE AND JOY. WE MUST GET INVOLVED AND STOP THIS SPIRIT OF DEATH FROM HOVERING OVER OUR CHILDREN, OUR NATION, AND THE WORLD. ONLY THE TRUTH OF JESUS CHRIST AND BECOMING ONE WITH HIM CAN SET THEM FREE. OUR MISSION IS TO SATURATE ALL OF MANKIND WITH THE TRUTH OF JESUS CHRIST, TO SOW THE SPIRIT OF LIFE, JESUS CHRIST THE ANSWER ETERNAL LIFE, AND SET FREE ALL OF CREATION FROM THE SPIRIT OF DEATH.

HOW YOU CAN HELP

NOW, I WANT TO TALK TO YOU ABOUT THE HOLY SPIRIT'S PLAN TO TAKE THE TRUTH OF THE GOSPEL TO OUR NATION AND THE WORLD. FIRST, LETS TALK ABOUT THE 15 SECOND VIDEO YOU SAW AT THE BEGINNING, OF THIS WEBSITE. GOD HAS OPENED A DOOR AND THIS VIDEO WILL BE PUT IN THE THEATERS ACROSS

THIS NATION. THIS VIDEO WILL PLAY BEFORE EVERY MOVIE, A PREVIEW OF THE TRUTH OF JESUS CHRIST. THIS VIDEO NEEDS TO PLAY IN EVERY TOWN ACROSS THIS NATION, ALONG WITH BILLBOARDS OF JESUS CHRIST THE ANSWER ETERNAL LIFE. EVERYWHERE YOU GO, YOU WOULD SEE JESUS CHRIST AND HIS MESSAGE. I CAN SEE SIGNS EVERYWHERE, SIDES OF TRACTOR AND TRAILERS DISPLAYING THE MESSAGE ACROSS THE NATION. BILLBOARDS IN ALL OUR CITIES, ESPECIALLY WASHINGTON DC. THIS VIDEO AND MESSAGE WILL BE SENT TO EVERY MEMBER OF CONGRESS, BOTH HOUSE AND SENATE, WHITE HOUSE AND OTHERS IN DC, AND ALL GOVERNORS OF ALL THE STATES. THIS MESSAGE WILL BE EVENTUALLY SENT TO THE HEAD OF ALL THE NATIONS. THIS MESSAGE OF TRUTH WILL BE BROADCAST ON SOCIAL MEDIA, RADIO, AND TV, AND SEMINARS ACROSS THE NATION. EVERYTHING ON THIS WEBSITE, CAN BE DOWNLOADED FOR FREE, THE MANUAL, THE BILLBOARDS, THE STICKERS, ETC. EVERYONE SHOULD HAVE HIS SIGNS, AND USE THE STICKERS ON EVERY PIECE OF MAIL THAT IS SENT OUT. WE WANT TO SATURATE THE WORLD, BOMBARD OUR CHILDREN WITH THE MESSAGE OF JESUS CHRIST, HIS LIFE, LOVE, PEACE, AND JOY. CHOOSE LIFE NOT DEATH. THIS WILL BE ACCOMPLISHED BY PEOPLE LIKE YOURSELVES GETTING AHOLD OF THIS REVELATION. THIS IS FORETOLD BY HABAKKUK, WRITE THE VISION, MAKE IT PLAIN UPON TABLES, THAT HE MAY RUN THAT READETH IT. GOD WILL BRING HIS VISION TO PASS. THERE ARE MANY WAYS, EXAMPLE, YOU GET INVOLVED AND HELP YOUR PASTOR/CHURCH IN YOUR TOWN, PAY FOR THE TIME THAT THE VIDEO RUNS IN YOUR LOCAL THEATER. AT THE SAME TIME THE CHURCH PUTS UP BILLBOARDS, AND SIGNS IN FRONT OF THE CHURCH FOR ALL PASSING BY TO SEE, THIS ALONE WOULD HELP SATURATE OUR NATION. YOUR CHURCH DOWNLOADS AND OR PURCHASES THIS BOOK (SOON TO BE AVAILABLE AT AMAZON) AND HANDS THEM OUT TO THE PEOPLE IN YOUR TOWN, AND GIVES THEM STICKERS. THE KIDS CAN PUT THEM ON THEIR PERSONAL ITEMS, SCHOOL, ETC. AND THE ADULTS ON THEIR MAIL. YOUR CHURCH COULD ORDER T-SHIRTS FROM OUR WEBSITE WITH THE LOGO JESUS

CHRIST THE ANSWER ETERNAL LIFE, AND GIVE THEM OUT, THE KIDS COULD WEAR THEM TO SCHOOL. WHAT IF EVERY KID IN YOUR TOWN HAD A FREE T-SHIRT TO WEAR PROCLAIMING THE GOSPEL MESSAGE. THERE ARE MANY WAYS GOD WILL WORK TO AWAKEN THE YOUTH, AND ADULTS OF OUR NATION AND THE WORLD TO THE TRUTH OF THE GOSPEL OF JESUS CHRIST. WE NEED TO SATURATE THE ENVIRONMENT, IN ALL PHASES, WITH THE KNOWLEDGE OF JESUS CHRIST, CHOOSE LIFE NOT DEATH. WE NEED YOU TO STEP UP TO THE PLATE AND START SPREADING THE TRUTH IN YOUR HOME TOWN TO YOUR FAMILIES AND YOUR NEIGHBORS. WE NEED TO FIND A WAY TO GET EVERYONE TO THIS WEBSITE, THIS WILL LEAD THEM TO THE TEACHING OF THE TRUTH OF THE GOSPEL OF JESUS CHRIST. THE HOLY SPIRIT HAS MADE IT CLEAR THAT WHEN THIS IS ACCOMPLISHED, OUR NATION WILL GREATLY BE CHANGED, AND THE NATIONS OF THE WORLD WILL BE CHANGED BY THE TRUTH, AND THE PEOPLE WILL BE SET FREE. NOW, IF THE HOLY SPIRIT IS LEADING YOU TO HELP WITH HIS PLAN, TO HELP ALL PEOPLE TO CHOOSE LIFE AND NOT DEATH, PLEASE SEND US YOUR THOUGHTS, YOUR IDEAS ON HOW THIS WILL BE ACCOMPLISHED AND YOU CAN DONATE ON OUR WEBSITE, chooselifenotdeath.com. YOU CAN ALSO DONATE TO ETERNAL LIFE COVENANT, AT PO BOX 755 BANNER ELK, NC 28604. WE NEED PARTNERS TO JOIN WITH US TO SHARE THE LIFE, LOVE AND ACCEPTANCE OF JESUS CHRIST WITH OUR NATION AND THE NATIONS OF THE WORLD. THANK YOU IN ADVANCE FOR YOUR HELP IN TAKING THE GOSPEL MESSAGE OF THE KINGDOM TO ALL THE WORLD. ETERNAL LIFE COVENANT IS NOT A 501C3. LET US ALL CHOOSE LIFE AND SPEAK LIFE NOT DEATH!

ABOUT THE AUTHOR....

PASTOR JAMES M HEATON III IS A THIRD-GENERATION PASTOR, TEACHER, AND WORSHIP LEADER. JAMES HEATON SR. STARTED, BUILT, AND PREACHED IN EIGHTEEN DIFFERENT CHURCHES IN THE MOUNTAINS OF WESTERN NORTH CAROLINA. IN THE LATE 1800'S AND EARLY 1900'S, JAMES HEATON JR. AND JAMES HEATON III FOLLOWED SUIT STARTING MORE CHURCHES AND CAMPUS MINISTRIES. NOW THE HOLY SPIRIT, THROUGH PASTOR JAMES, IS TEACHING YOU THE DEEP REVELATIONS OF HOW TO SOW THE SPIRIT OF LIFE, JESUS CHRIST THE ANSWER ETERNAL LIFE INTO ALL THE WORLD AND SET FREE ALL OF CREATION FROM THE SPIRIT OF DEATH.

DAILY PRAYER...BELIEVE & RECEIVE

DAILY READ YOUR BIBLE, TRUST, OBEY AND ACT ON GOD'S HOLY LIVING WORD OF TRUTH.

DAILY CONFESS AND REPENT...

"JESUS CHRIST, I CONFESS AND REPENT OF MY SIN (AGREEMENT WITH THE SPIRIT OF DEATH), THAT WOULD KEEP YOU FROM ABIDING IN ME AND ME FROM ABIDING IN YOU. HOLY SPIRIT, JESUS CHRIST, FATHER GOD, CLEANSE ME OF ALL UNRIGHTEOUSNESS, SET ME FREE, GIVE ME YOUR PEACE, LIFT ME INTO YOUR PRESENCE, INTO YOUR MARVELOUS LIGHT, INTO ETERNAL LIFE ON EARTH AS IT IS IN HEAVEN. THE SAME LOVE THAT CREATED ME IS RESTORING ME NOW, RESTORATION OF ALL IN ALL AS IF IT NEVER HAPPENED. THANK YOU JESUS FOR SETTING ME FREE."

DAILY COMMUNION...

JESUS CHRIST MADE A WAY WHERE THERE WAS NO WAY. TO BECOME **ONE** WITH JESUS CHRIST, HE INSTITUTED COMMUNION WITH HIS OWN BODY AND HIS OWN BLOOD TO SET YOU FREE. THE HOLY SPIRIT, THROUGH COMMUNION, LIFTS YOU UP INTO HIS PRESENCE AND SEATS YOU IN HEAVENLY PLACES, ETERNAL LIFE. THIS COMMUNION IS BETWEEN YOU AND JESUS CHRIST ONLY!

NO PASTOR OR PRIEST IS REQUIRED. ALSO, ANY FOOD AND DRINK IS ACCEPTABLE.

"THIS IS HIS BODY, THE BREAD OF LIFE, BROKEN FOR ME, AND THIS IS HIS BLOOD, THE BLOOD OF THE NEW COVENANT, THE ETERNAL LIFE COVENANT, A FRESH TRANSFUSION OF GOD'S DNA, WASHES AWAY THE SPIRIT OF DEATH, AND GIVES ME AUTHORITY OVER DEATH. THANK YOU JESUS FOR SETTING ME FREE."

DAILY TESTIMONY...

"I AM A NEW CREATURE FILLED WITH THE HOLY SPIRIT OF ALMIGHTY GOD, THE SPIRIT OF ETERNAL LIFE, SEATED IN HEAVENLY PLACES WITH JESUS CHRIST, MY LORD AND SAVIOR. I AM NOT SUBJECT TO NATURAL LAW, NATURAL LAW IS SUBJECT TO ME. I AM NOT OF THIS WORLD, **I HAVE AUTHORITY OVER DEATH, *DEATH HAS NO HOLD ON ME*.** I AM A TRUE SON OR DAUGHTER OF GOD, MADE IN THE IMAGE OF GOD, LOVED, ACCEPTED, AND RESTORED WITH ETERNAL LIFE ON EARTH AS IT IS IN HEAVEN. I AM GOING TO LIVE ON THIS EARTH HEALTHY, WHOLE, PROSPEROUS, BLESSED, REGENERATED AND RESTORED, IN LOVE, PEACE, AND JOY, SPIRIT, SOUL AND BODY BLAMELESS, UNTIL JESUS RETURNS. AND HE WILL FIND ME SOWING THE SPIRIT OF LIFE, JESUS CHRIST THE ANSWER ETERNAL LIFE INTO ALL THE WORLD, AND SETTING FREE ALL OF CREATION FROM THE SPIRIT OF DEATH, AND THEN I AM GOING TO LIVE, RULE AND REIGN WITH HIM FOREVER. THANK YOU JESUS FOR SETTING ME FREE! AMEN!"

THE LIGHT OF THE REVELATION OF THE KNOWLEDGE OF JESUS CHRIST IS SHINING BRIGHTLY!
THE DOORS OF HEAVEN ARE OPENING AND GOD IS BLESSING HIS SONS AND DAUGHTERS WITH HIS KNOWLEDGE. THIS KNOWLEDGE IS BEING REVEALED TO US ON A DAILY BASIS. YOU WILL BE ABLE TO RECEIVE THESE REVELATIONS OF KNOWLEDGE BY FOLLOWING US ON OUR PODCASTS AT: www.chooselifenotdeath.com.

PUBLISHER'S DESCRIPTION......

YOU HAVE AUTHORITY OVER DEATH.... DEATH HAS NO HOLD ON YOU!

THIS BOOK IS A HOW-TO MANUAL THAT WILL TEACH YOU HOW TO BECOME ONE IN ETERNAL LIFE WITH JESUS CHRIST, OUR LORD AND SAVIOR. JESUS IS ETERNAL LIFE, THIS IS NOT WHAT HE HAS, BUT WHO HE IS, THEREFORE, HE CAN GIVE IT TO YOU. WHY? BECAUSE HE LOVES YOU REGARDLESS OF WHAT YOU BELIEVE OR WHAT YOU HAVE DONE. JESUS LOVES EVERYONE THE SAME. JESUS WILL NEVER ACCUSE OR CONDEMN YOU, HE WILL SET YOU FREE, JOHN 3:16. THIS BOOK WILL TEACH YOU HOW TO BE SEATED WITH JESUS IN HEAVENLY PLACES, AND SEE WHAT IS REAL AND WHAT IS NOT REAL, WHAT IS TRUE AND WHAT IS NOT TRUE. THIS BOOK WILL TAKE YOU INTO THE DEEPER TRUTHS OF GOD CONCERNING THE POWER IN DAILY READING GOD'S HOLY LIVING WORD OF TRUTH, THE HOLY BIBLE, DAILY PRAYER, BAPTISM OF WATER, DAILY COMMUNION, DAILY TESTIMONY

AND BAPTISM OF THE HOLY SPIRIT. COMMUNION DOES NOT REQUIRE A PASTOR OR PRIEST, THIS IS YOUR PERSONAL INTIMACY WITH JESUS CHRIST. THIS BOOK TEACHES YOU HOW TO SPEAK FORTH AND MINISTER WITH JESUS IN THE SPIRITUAL GIFTS. TO HELP YOU GRASP THE FACT THAT WITH JESUS YOU HAVE OVERCOME SIN, AGREEMENT WITH THE SPIRIT OF DEATH. YOU HAVE BEEN RESTORED SPIRIT, SOUL, AND BODY WITH ETERNAL LIFE ON EARTH AS IT IS IN HEAVEN. WHEN YOU TRULY BECOME ONE WITH JESUS AS HE IS ONE WITH THE FATHER YOU ARE NO LONGER PART OF THIS WORLD, YOU ARE SEATED IN HEAVENLY PLACES. YOU ARE NOT SUBJECT TO NATURAL LAW, NATURAL LAW IS SUBJECT TO YOU. YOU HAVE AUTHORITY OVER CREATION, REMEMBER THE DEVIL IS A CREATED BEING, THEREFORE YOU HAVE AUTHORITY OVER THE DEVIL, SO DEATH HAS NO HOLD ON YOU. YOU MUST UNDERSTAND THAT YOU ARE EITHER IN LIFE OR DEATH ALL THE TIME. THIS BOOK WILL NOT ONLY TEACH YOU HOW TO STAY IN LIFE, RESTORE AND REGENERATE, BUT ALSO HOW TO OPERATE WITH JESUS IN HIS MIRACLES OF LOVE. EVERY BELIEVER FILLED WITH THE HOLY SPIRIT, THE SPIRIT OF ETERNAL LIFE, HAS THE AUTHORITY AND ABILITY TO MINISTER WITH JESUS TO BREAK AND OVERCOME THE SPIRIT OF DEATH OFF OF PEOPLE'S LIVES, SET THEM FREE, SEE THEM HEALED, REGENERATED AND RESTORED, SPIRIT, SOUL, AND BODY. THIS BOOK WILL TEACH YOU HOW TO BELIEVE AND RECEIVE. WAKE UP, CATCH THIS: DO NOT BELIEVE WHAT YOU SEE, SEE WHAT YOU BELIEVE! REMEMBER, BY HIS STRIPES YOU ARE HEALED, FAITH IS SIMPLY AGREEING WITH JESUS CHRIST. OUR MISSION IS TO SOW THE SPIRIT OF LIFE, JESUS CHRIST THE ANSWER ETERNAL LIFE INTO ALL THE WORLD AND SET FREE ALL OF CREATION FROM THE SPIRIT OF DEATH. BUCKLE UP, WITH JESUS IN YOU, YOU ARE THE LIGHT IN THIS DARK WORLD, GREATER IS HE THAT IS IN YOU THAN

HE THAT IS IN THE WORLD. JESUS IS THE WAY, THE TRUTH, AND THE LIFE, (ETERNAL LIFE), AND NO ONE COMES TO THE FATHER BUT BY HIM, JOHN 14:6. YOU TOO CAN BE A PART OF THIS MISSION UNTIL JESUS RETURNS IN HIS GLORY TO SET UP HIS ONE WORLD ORDER, HIS KINGDOM OF PEACE, LOVE, AND GREAT JOY FOR ALL PEOPLE, JUST AS THE ANGELS ANNOUNCED AT HIS COMING.

30-DAY DEVOTIONAL
DAY 1

In the beginning was the Word, and the Word was with God, and the Word was God. John 1:1

DAY 2

All things were made by him; and without
him was not any thing made that was made.
John 1:3

DAY 3

For the law was given by Moses, but grace
and truth came by Jesus Christ.
John 1:17

DAY 4

And I knew him not: but he that sent me to
baptize with water, the same said unto me,
Upon whom thou shalt see the Spirit
descending, and remaining on him, the
same is he which baptizeth with the Holy
Ghost.
John 1:33

DAY 5

That whosoever believeth in him should not
perish, but have eternal life.
John 3:15

For God so loved the world, that he gave his
only begotten Son, that whosoever
believeth in him should not perish, but have
everlasting life.
John 3:16

DAY 7

For God sent not his Son into the world to
condemn the world; but that the world
through him might be saved.
John 3:17

DAY 8

He that believeth on the Son hath
everlasting life: and he that believeth not
the Son shall not see life; but the wrath of
God abideth on him.
John 3:36

DAY 9

God is a Spirit: and they that worship him
must worship him in spirit and in truth.
John 4:24

Jesus answered and said unto him, Verily, verily, I say unto thee, Except a man be born again, he cannot see the kingdom of God.
John 3:3

DAY 11

Jesus answered, Verily, verily, I say unto
thee, Except a man be born of water and of
the Spirit, he cannot enter into the kingdom
of God.
John 3:5

DAY 12

That which is born of the flesh is flesh; and
that which is born of the Spirit is spirit.
John 3:6

Then answered Jesus and said unto them, Verily, verily, I say unto you, The Son can do nothing of himself, but what he seeth the Father do: for what things soever he doeth, these also doeth the Son likewise.
John 5:19

DAY 14

For the Father judgeth no man, but hath
committed all judgment unto the Son:
John 5:22

That all men should honour the Son, even as they honour the Father. He that honoureth not the Son honoureth not the Father which hath sent him.

John 5:23

DAY 16

Verily, verily, I say unto you, He that
heareth my word, and believeth on him
that sent me, hath everlasting life, and shall
not come into condemnation; but is passed
from death unto life.
John 5:24

Search the scriptures; for in them ye think
ye have eternal life: and they are they
which testify of me.
John 5:39

DAY 18

For the bread of God is he which cometh
down from heaven, and giveth life unto the
world.
John 6:33

DAY 19

And Jesus said unto them, I am the bread of life: he that cometh to me shall never hunger; and he that believeth on me shall never thirst.
John 6:35

And this is the will of him that sent me, that
every one which seeth the Son, and
believeth on him, may have everlasting life:
and I will raise him up at the last day.
John 6:40

Verily, verily, I say unto you, He that believeth on me hath everlasting life.
John 6:47

DAY 22

I am the living bread which came down
from heaven: if any man eat of this bread,
he shall live for ever: and the bread that I
will give is my flesh, which I will give for the
life of the world.
John 6:51

Then Jesus said unto them, Verily, verily, I say unto you, Except ye eat the flesh of the Son of man, and drink his blood, ye have no life in you.
John 6:53

DAY 24

Whoso eateth my flesh, and drinketh my
blood, hath eternal life; and I will raise him
up at the last day.
John 6:54

He that eateth my flesh, and drinketh my
blood, dwelleth in me, and I in him.
John 6:56

It is the spirit that quickeneth; the flesh
profiteth nothing: the words that I speak
unto you, they are spirit, and they are life.
John 6:63

I said therefore unto you, that ye shall die in your sins: for if ye believe not that I am he, ye shall die in your sins.
John 8:24

DAY 28

And ye shall know the truth, and the truth
shall make you free.
John 8:32

If the Son therefore shall make you free, ye
shall be free indeed.
John 8:36

Jesus said unto her, I am the resurrection, and the life: he that believeth in me, though he were dead, yet shall he live:
John 11:25

And whosoever liveth and believeth in me shall never die. Believest thou this?
John 11:26

Jesus saith unto him, I am the way, the truth, and the life: no man cometh unto the Father, but by me.
John 14:6

"THE ANSWER" – A POEM

"LOOK AT THIS WORLD
RUNNING TO AND FRO
NOT KNOWING WHERE TO GO
JESUS IS THE ANSWER
TO ALL THEIR WOES
ONLY JESUS CAN SET THEIR HEARTS AFLAME
ONLY JESUS CAN SET THEIR SPIRITS FREE
ONLY JESUS CAN BRING PEACE INTO THEIR
TROUBLED SOULS
ONLY JESUS, JESUS CHRIST, LORD GOD ALMIGHTY
THE ANSWER!"

COMPOSED BY THE HOLY SPIRIT
AUGUST 1ST, 2007
PASTOR JAMES M HEATON III
BANNER ELK, NC

Made in the USA
Coppell, TX
22 September 2020

38559039R00066